Plugging into God's Story:

A practical introduction to reading and understanding the Bible

By Kevin Goodrich, O.P.

Copyright © 2007 by Kevin Goodrich O.P.

Plugging into God's Story
by Kevin Goodrich O.P.

Printed in the United States of America

ISBN 978-1-60266-148-6

All rights reserved solely by the author. The author guarantees all contents are original and do not infringe upon the legal rights of any other person or work. No part of this book may be reproduced in any form without the permission of the author. The views expressed in this book are not necessarily those of the publisher.

Unless otherwise indicated, Bible quotations are taken from the New International Version, Study Bible. Copyright © 2000 by Zondervan.

www.xulonpress.com

I have had the privilege of teaching the Bible to people of all ages: from children in Sunday School, to teenagers on retreats, men and women in adult classes, and senior adults in prayer meetings. This book is dedicated to them. Without their constant questions, their faith, and their insights, my own knowledge of the Bible, and its connection to daily living, would be greatly reduced.

Contents

Introduction ix

How To Use This Book xii

Daily Bible Readings 14

Conclusion 215

Introduction

The Bible continues to hold the record as the world's all time best seller. You can find the Bible in hands of commuters on public transportation in the developed world, as well as in the hands of a farmer in the plains of Africa. The Bible, while originally written in Hebrew and Greek, has been translated into more languages than any other book ever written. The Bible is studied by many undergraduate students in college because of its standing as one of the greatest literary works every written in the history of humanity. If you live in the United States, you know, it's not unusual to hear the Bible referenced in cultural debates about the morality of war, abortion, sexuality, or science.

The Bible is an integral part of Western Civilization not only in its religious contexts but in its wider literary, social, and cultural spheres as well. There is a movement among some educators to teach the Bible in high school. This isn't an attempt to bring religion into schools, but to give students access to some of the foundational literature of America and the Western World. References to the Bible are found throughout history in the works of such important cultural figures as William Shakespeare, Mark Twain, and Arthur Miller. Without an understanding of the Bible, many authors, as well as events in American history, cannot be fully understood. Knowing the Bible will enable you to better understand culture, literature, and the history of your own society.

Beyond Literature: The Bible as God's Word

More important, knowing the Bible gives you the opportunity to develop your own personal spirituality and relationship with God. The Bible is the sacred book for followers of Jesus Christ, commonly known as Christians today. Whether you're a Christian or not, the Bible offers unique insights into the heart of human nature, the way relationships work, and the ultimate purpose of life. The Bible itself can be thought of as a collection of books brought together in one sacred library. There is a wide range of genres, or types of books in the Bible, including history, poetry, story, and law. This is important to realize when trying to make sense of what the Bible is saying. For example, you wouldn't read a romance novel the same way you would read a science essay. You expect different sorts of things from each kind of writing. Each writing might convey things that are true about human living, but do so in a different way. Likewise, if you are reading a poetic section of Scriptures (Psalms for example) you should read it differently from a book of history (1 Kings for example).

It's also important to know that the Bible was written by a number of authors. Scholars debate about the exact number, but general estimates put it in the range of forty different human authors, who wrote the different books of the Bible over a long period of time. Some of the earliest parts of the Bible in the Old Testament may have first been written down over 3000 years ago (1000 BC), while the newest parts of the Bible in the New Testament may be have been written down in a little less than 2000 years ago (100 AD).

During your lifetime you've probably heard the Bible described as being God's Word. You might have wondered, what does that mean exactly? There is considerable diversity among people of faith about the nature of the Bible. However, all of the positions held by different Christian churches about the Bible can be summarized by the following chart.

| HUMAN | BOTH | DIVINE |

Some Christian communities emphasize that the Bible was written by human beings. They tend to believe that the Bible is not so much God's Word as it is the reflections of humanity about its relationship with God. These types of churches would tend to be considered progressive theologically and would fall on the left side of the chart. Then there are Christian communities that tend to emphasize the divine nature of the Bible almost to the exclusion of the human side. These types of churches tend to be very conservative theologically and fall on the right side of the chart. Classically, over the centuries the traditional Christian position on the Bible has been to understand it has having both human and divine elements.

Understood this way, and this is the approach taken in this book, the Bible is recognized as having been written by human beings under the inspiration or special guidance of God. In other words, while human beings literally wrote the words of the Bible, God worked through these writers to convey timeless truths about Himself for all people and for all times. The authorship of the Bible can be best understood as a dual authorship between God and His people. The Bible is a way that you and I can receive guidance from God for our own individual lives by reading about the lives of God's people in history.

Reading the Bible for Life

At this point you probably have several questions about the Bible and how it works. However, the purpose of this book is not to explore the Bible from an academic or scholarly perspective, but to encourage you to read the Bible. Further, this book assumes that the Bible is highly practical for your life. Christianity understands God to be the master storyteller of the universe. The Bible provides us with the broad strokes of God's story for all life. Our job as individuals and faith communities is to figure out how the little stories and events of our own lives fit into the greater story of God. Yet, a real challenge for many of us is that we don't know the Bible. You might know some stories in the Bible or you might know very little about the Bible. In either case this book is designed to familiarize you with the basic storyline of the Bible from Genesis to Revelation.

As you read the Bible and this book you should always be asking yourself, "How does my personal story fit into this part of God's story?" Ultimately, by living out our lives in a Christian community (a local church) and engaging in Bible reading we can became aware of the special story that God has for our own lives. It is my hope that this book helps you begin to realize the kind of story God wants to co-author with you for your life.

How To Use This Book

The purpose of this book is to help you better understand the big picture of the Bible and God's story for life. This book takes the approach that the best way for you to better understand the Bible is to read it. There are 100 Bible passages that are highlighted in this book. I suggest that you read one Bible passage a day. In addition, to this book you'll need a Bible. I suggest you get a Bible translation that is easy to read and that includes study notes. If you don't have such a Bible, your local church or bookstore can help you to find one.

Each daily reading includes some background information to help you understand the passage as well as questions to help you think about the passage more critically. Each daily reading builds upon the previous readings to slowly increase your understanding of the Bible. You will find references to different parts of the Bible as you read the material in this book. For example, you might read at the end of a sentence or the section called "Related Bible Passages," Matthew 1:1-6. This is the shorthand format for referring to a specific section of the Bible. The Bible is divided into many books (in this case Matthew is being referenced), with chapters in each book (chapter 1 of Matthew in this case), and then into verses, or numbered sentences within each chapter (in this case verses 1-6 of chapter 1). These different references are included to help you expand your knowledge of how different parts of the Bible interact with each other.

Plugging into God's Story

In addition, you will find the following chart at the top of each daily reading:

Creation   Covenant   Christ   Church   Conclusion

This chart describes in broad strokes the major plot movements of God's story.

    Creation: This section of the Bible describes God's creation of the world and humanity.

    Covenant: This section of the Bible describes God's special promise and relationship with His people.

    Christ: This section of the Bible describes the life and work of Jesus the Christ.

    Church: This section of the Bible describes the early life of the Church.

    Conclusion: This section of the Bible describes the end of God's story for the universe.

As you progress through the daily readings, you will notice that beginning with Creation, the words on the chart will be highlighted. This is to help you orient yourself to the big picture of God's story. By the time you reach the end of the book all five of the words will be highlighted.

Lastly, you will notice that the daily reading includes a suggestion to "Pray for the Spirit's Insight." Prayer is an essential part of reading the Bible for spiritual understanding and growth. The Christian faith teaches that ultimately it is God's active presence, the Spirit, that helps us to know, experience, and understand Him. A simple prayer you could pray before reading the daily passage is this: "Lord speak to my life through the words of the Bible today."

If you've read this far, congratulations, you are now ready to start reading the Bible!

DAY 1

Scripture Reading: Genesis 1: 1-12

Creation   Covenant   Christ   Church   Conclusion

Overview: To understand the entire story of God revealed in the Bible, you must be familiar with the book of Genesis. All of the people and places described in the Scriptures are directly shaped by the events described in the first three chapters of the book of Genesis. Once you develop an ear and an eye for the language of the book of Genesis, you will be surprised to find echoes of Genesis throughout the rest of the Old Testament, as well as in the New Testament, and especially in the ministry of Jesus and the book of Revelation. The word genesis means, "beginning," and of course the book is so named, not only because it describes the creation of the world, but it tells the story of the first people who actively sought to follow the one God. The particular passage you will be reading today records God's work of shaping the universe in the first two days of creation.

Pray for the Spirit's Insight

Read the Passage

Understanding the Passage

What did this passage mean for the Jewish people thousands of years ago when it was first told orally and then written down?

What does this passage mean for people living in today's world?

What does the passage mean to you?

Questions for Further Consideration

Does this passage describe the beginning of God? Or does it describe the beginning of God's creation?

How does God appear to create things according to the passage?

Related Bible Passages

John 1: 1-5

DAY 2

Scripture Reading: Genesis 1: 13-25

Creation   Covenant   Christ   Church   Conclusion

Overview: The story of God's creation continues to unfold in today's passage from the book of Genesis. God creates the vast universe and all of its life by merely speaking, and when God speaks life is created. It is important to understand that the early chapters of Genesis were written to convey the truth that God is the source and creator of all life rather than to describe any specific scientific theory or explanation. This is not to say that Genesis does not describe actual reality, but that its primary purpose was to affirm God as the author, creator, and sustainer of all life. The creation accounts in Genesis describe the big picture of what God did in the beginning of creation's story. Sincere Christians may disagree as to whether God created the world in a literal six days or whether God used a process like evolution to create His masterpiece. The central thrust of today's reading is that God is not only the creator but the encourager of life.

Pray for the Spirit's Insight

Read the Passage

Understanding the Passage

What do you think is the significance of the repeated phrase, "And God saw that it was good" in this section of Genesis?

Do you see any potential conflict between God's blessings of the animals in verse 22 and how human civilization is currently taking care of the planet?

Questions for Further Consideration

If God created the entire universe, then God also created the other galaxies, planets, and solar systems. Why do you think God made such a vast universe?

Related Bible Passages

Psalm 148

DAY 3

Scripture Reading: Genesis 1: 26-31, Genesis 2:1-3

Creation   Covenant   Christ   Church   Conclusion

Overview: From the depths of the sea to the distant peaks of mountains Genesis tells us that God created them all. The ancient people who told and wrote down the Genesis stories would have been unaware of the vast abundance of microorganisms that exist which are invisible to the human eye. Likewise, they would have been unaware of the vast array of other galaxies in our universe. Yet, the fundamental truth that God is the creator of all things, whether as small as the one celled amoeba or as mammoth as the giant planet Jupiter, remains the same. The divine chorus that God continues to proclaim as He creates the world in all its complexity is that "it is good." All forms of life and even inanimate creations are given timeless value by God's declaration that they are good. This declaration tells us that nothing in this world is without inherent worth and that all things are deserving of proper care and stewardship. In today's passage we read about the sixth day of creation where the Creator creates human beings in the image of God.

Pray for the Spirit's Insight

Read the Passage

Understanding the Passage

What does it mean that man and woman were created in the image of God?

Verse 26 describes the leadership role given to humanity over the planet. Do you see this as a mandate for human beings to dominate the creation or to take care of it?

Questions for Further Consideration

In most Bible translation verse 26 includes language like "let us" and "in our image," who is this us or we?

Related Bible Passages

Psalm 8

DAY 4

Scripture Reading: Genesis 2: 4-17

Creation   Covenant   Christ   Church   Conclusion

Overview: While all of life is sacred and to be valued, human beings were created in the likeness, in the image of God. This means that somehow who we are as people reflects the divine life of God. In Genesis a greater emphasis is placed on the collective state of all men and woman, reflecting the image of God, rather than on individual men and women being image bearers by themselves. It is true every person bears the image of God but in a real way we better reflect who God is in community. The plural references that God uses in the previous passage may well refer to the divine community, itself such as the angels of heaven or the persons of the Holy Trinity. Moving deeper into chapter two of Genesis we find what seems to be another story of creation. While Genesis chapter 1 highlights the big picture of God's creative activity, the story in Genesis chapter 2 highlights the details related to God's creative activity with special attention being given to the creation of humanity.

Pray for the Spirit's Insight

Read the Passage

Understanding the Passage

What is it that finally brings man to life in this passage?

Notice how this creation story situates these ancient events in a particular part of the known world. What part of the world serves as the backdrop for this story?

Questions for Further Consideration

Does verse 15 contain any implications for how you are to relate to the planet?

Do you think God's command in verse 17 is a reasonable one? Why or why not?

Related Bible Passages

Psalm 8

DAY 5

Scripture Reading: Genesis 2: 18-25

Creation Covenant Christ Church Conclusion

Overview: The story of God's creation can now be situated in the geography of this world in the Middle East. The Tigris and Euphrates rivers can still be found, touched, and crossed in such countries as Iraq, Turkey, and Syria. While the language of Genesis is poetic and intended to convey cosmic truths, the inclusion of actual places serves as a spiritual anchor, reminding us that this powerful Creator God is actually involved in the real world that we live in. The man that God creates is formed out of the dust of the earth but is made alive through the breath of God. To live from a Biblical perspective is to be a man or woman who lives because of the power of God. Adam is situated in the Garden of Eden, a place of beauty and intimacy with God. Interestingly, even in paradise Adam is not left to do whatever he wants in some sort of permanent spiritual vacation. Rather Adam is entrusted with the work of taking care of the garden. All of Adam's needs are provided for and he is free to live in communion with God and His creation. The only restriction on Adam's freedom is the warning to not eat the fruit on the tree of the knowledge of good and evil. This seems a wise warning since according to verse 17, to eat of the fruit will result in Adam's death. In today's passage the story of creation continues with the creating of the first woman, Eve.

Pray for the Spirit's Insight

Read the Passage

Understanding the Passage

What implications for your life does God's statement in verse 17 hold?

Questions for Further Consideration

Why were Adam and Eve not ashamed that they were naked?

Is there any significance to the fact that God let Adam name the animals?

Related Bible Passages

Matthew 19:4

DAY 6

Scripture Reading: Genesis 3: 1-7

Creation   Covenant   Christ   Church   Conclusion

Overview: Human beings were created in the image of God, and in the Christian faith God is understood to be a perfect community unto Himself; that perfect community being the Father, the Son, and the Holy Spirit. God's statement that, "it is not good for the man to be alone," tells us that human beings are literally designed for relationship. Human beings can be nurtured by many relationships including the companionship of God's other living creations. Yet, as Adam discovered, the companionship of animals was not enough to complete him as a human being. Our identities as women and men are good things established by and blessed by God. We were designed for each other, not only in the sense of sexual expression and romantic commitment, but to be "helpers" or friends to each other in God's world. To be naked in our world is to feel vulnerable, exposed, and unsafe. In God's paradise Adam and Eve felt safe, secure, and content. They were naked, not only physically but emotionally and spiritually, to each other and to God. In today's passage all of this changes because of a decision that Adam and Eve make that shatters the perfect world of paradise and allows sin to become a part of the human condition. Classically, this passage in the Bible has been called, "The Fall of Man."

Pray for the Spirit's Insight

Read the Passage

Understanding the Passage

How does the snake deceive Adam and Eve into eating the fruit?

Why do you think Adam and Eve ate the fruit? What was their motivation?

Questions for Further Consideration

What does it mean that Adam and Eve's eyes were opened?

What changed that caused Adam and Eve to feel ashamed of their nakedness?

Related Bible Passages

Romans 5:12-14

DAY 7

Scripture Reading: Genesis 3: 8-24

Creation   Covenant   Christ   Church   Conclusion

Overview: In the Garden of Eden the man and woman knew nothing about division, hatred, or strife. They literally had no knowledge of evil except to know it was something that was not in alignment with God. The snake, who has been understood to be Satan by generations of Christians, did not blatantly tell the first couple to disobey God's command. Rather, in a strike of brilliance the snake questioned whether God really said not to eat from the tree in the first place. The snake challenged God's integrity and suggested to the first man and woman that God was really holding back something good from them. Adam and Eve were apparently convinced by the snake's slippery argument because they ate the fruit of the forbidden tree, seeking a delicious snack along with the wisdom it would provide. Ultimately, they chose their own ways, desires, and motivations over God. Adam and Eve represent humanity and they jointly, were responsible for the act which led to the great disconnect between humanity and divinity. This disconnect which we will learn more about in today's passage opened the eyes of Adam and Eve to a world where choosing against God and each other became possible. Until this point there was no fear of God in the human race, but today's passage shows us that after the Fall fear became a part of the relationship between God and people.

Pray for the Spirit's Insight

Read the Passage

Understanding the Passage

When asked by God about the fruit, how do Adam and Eve react?

What are some of the consequences for Adam and Eve for eating the fruit?

Questions for Further Consideration

Does this passage provide any insight into why our world is so broken?

Have you ever found yourself behaving like Adam and Eve?

Related Bible Passages

James 1:13-15

DAY 8

Scripture Reading: Genesis 4: 1-7

Creation   Covenant   Christ   Church   Conclusion

Overview: Paradise, the place where perfect relationship between God and humanity was possible, is no more. The consequences for the first man and woman for choosing their own ways over God's ways are vast and encompassing. All of life is now changed. The earth will still produce food for humanity but at great cost in labor, pain, and time. New life in the form of human children will take place in this new fallen world, but only after the woman has endured increased pain and agony. The perfect partnership between Adam and Eve as helpers and lovers to each other is now also scarred. Relationships between men and women will now be marked with the desire to control and manipulate one another. The world, once so vibrant in the Garden of Eden, is now a shadow of its former self, still created good by God but now out of alignment with God's full purposes. Free will, which was the most precious gift that God gave Adam and Eve, resulted in the fallen and broken world we live in today. Disease, disaster, and destruction are all possible in this sort of world that was not fully connected to its God. It is at this very moment that the whole of creation began to yearn to return to Eden, but it will be many thousands of years before God sends the person who could reconnect humanity back to God and give even the fallen creation the hope that one day all would be made new. In today's passage we see the damaging effects of the Fall upon human relationships.

Pray for the Spirit's Insight

Read the Passage

Understanding the Passage

Why did God not accept Cain's offering? Does the passage give you any clues?

Why do you think Cain reacted so negatively to God's decision?

Questions for Further Consideration

Can you relate to Cain at all? Have you ever felt God didn't accept your offering?

Related Bible Passages

Hebrews 11:4

DAY 9

Scripture Reading: Genesis 4: 8-15

Creation   Covenant   Christ   Church   Conclusion

Overview: Humanity's new self-awareness of it's separation from God was symbolized by Adam and Eve's shame at their nakedness. Once the first human beings had rebelled against God, a chain of rebellion was set in motion that we encounter in the dark story of Cain and Abel. Both are sons of the first couple who could tell them stories about life with God in the Garden of Eden. Yet, the only world that Cain and Abel knew was a post-garden world. While life was challenging it was still good and humanity still sought to be in relationship with God. The passage does not give us a clear answer as to why God found Abel's offering pleasing and Cain's offering unacceptable. However, Cain's reaction is telling in that he gets angry and refuses to listen to God's encouragement and advice. Perhaps Cain gave his offering out of a sense of duty, or a sense of competition with Abel, but whatever his motivation, was it was not an honest one to please God. God warns Cain that sin is crouching at his door. Cain is in a potentially dangerous state of being because the sin that is brewing inside of him could unleash itself in something hideous and destructive. Sin, that which separates us from God, each other, and ultimately ourselves is ready to give birth in Cain. Today's reading records the unleashing of that sin from Cain's heart into Cain's behavior.

Pray for the Spirit's Insight

Read the Passage

Understanding the Passage

Are there any hints that Cain preplanned his brother's murder in this passage?

Do you hear echoes from earlier passages of Genesis in today's reading?

Questions for Further Consideration

God knew what Cain did so why did He bother asking ,"where is your brother?"

Have you ever noticed a tendency to wander away from God when you have sinned or fallen from God's ways in your life?

Related Bible Passages

Matthew 23:35

DAY 10

Scripture Reading: Genesis 6: 9-22

Creation   Covenant   Christ   Church   Conclusion

Overview: The tragedy of sin is fully unleashed in the betrayal of God and family in the murderous actions of Cain against his brother Abel. Already the careful reader will hear echoes of the first transgression against God by Adam and Eve in the encounter between God and Cain. Cain's parents sought to evade responsibility for eating the forbidden fruit by blaming it on each other and the snake. Cain does not take God's gracious offer to come clean about his actions but instead evades responsibility by saying, "am I my brother's keeper?" While the Scripture is not conclusive, it does appear that Cain premeditated this murder when he invited his brother to go out into the field. Sin has not only made crimes of passion possible, but it also created the possibility for calculated sin planned ahead of time, and executed with intentional will and desire, to be a part of the behavior of humanity. Further, once Cain has so grievously separated himself from God and his family, he is doomed to wander without a place to call home. In our own lives, when we separate ourselves from God by our actions or by refusing God's gracious invitation to confess our brokenness, we often find ourselves in a season of spiritual wandering with no place to call home. Unfortunately, as the descendents of Adam and Eve continued to multiply and increase on the earth so did their capability for sin. Just prior to today's passage the Bible describes God as grieved about His creations and their terrible rebellion against His ways. The situation on planet earth isn't very good and God is considering starting the whole creation process over. This is where we find ourselves in today's reading.

Pray for the Spirit's Insight

Read the Passage

Understanding the Passage

What are the reasons that God desires to wipe out the human race?

Questions for Further Consideration

If you were Noah how would you feel if God told you to build the Ark?

Related Bible Passages

Matthew 24:37

DAY 11

Scripture Reading: Genesis 9: 1-11

Creation   Covenant   Christ   Church   Conclusion

Overview: At this point in God's story we are still in the beginning of history where the earliest interactions between humanity and God took place. Once sin entered the human landscape it spread rapidly like a disease, and we find God grieving over His creations to the point of planning to start creation anew with Noah and his family. As contemporary people we are challenged by the idea of a God who would wipe out His entire creation in order to start over again. However, just consider that a few generations ago human beings were created in the first place. Adam and Eve had walked with God in the Garden of Eden. Even after the Fall, humans seemed to have an intimate knowledge of God. Then, very quickly after the murder of Abel by Cain, humanity seems to abandon God altogether. It is at this point that God calls Noah to build a gigantic ship, an ark, on which a remnant, a faithful portion of humanity, will be saved to start the creation process anew after the flood. It's hard to know how Noah felt except it seems likely that he suffered great ridicule from his neighbors and wider community. Just imagine building a cruise liner in your front yard and telling everyone that God told you to do it! In our own lives the flood waters of despair, activity, or darkness can be overwhelming, but we must trust that God will provide an ark to get us through the flood to a new place with dry ground. After forty days and nights of rain and flood waters, Noah and his family come out of the ark onto dry ground. It is here that we encounter God making a formal agreement with human beings, a promise, which in the Bible is often called a covenant.

Pray for the Spirit's Insight

Read the Passage

Understanding the Passage

What does God promise Noah and his family?

Do you hear any echoes of previous passages in Genesis in this text?

Questions for Further Consideration

Has God ever given you an ark to get you through a difficult time in your life?

Related Bible Passages

Hebrews 11:7

DAY 12

Scripture Reading: Genesis 11: 1-8

Creation   Covenant   Christ   Church   Conclusion

Overview: God blesses Noah and his family with words that echo God's blessings of humanity in Genesis 1:28, "Be fruitful and increase in number and fill the earth." The flood waters have abated and God has promised to never flood the entire earth again. The rainbows that you and I see are a continuing reminder of God's covenant with Noah and his ancestors. God entrusts His creation to Noah and his descendents by giving them free rein to live off of the lands. However, God is careful to instruct Noah's family that they are to respect animal life by not eating meat that still has blood in it. In other words, while human beings have charge of the earth, they are not to recklessly take advantage of its resources. The covenant with Noah also affirms the inherent dignity and value of every human being by once again declaring that human beings are created in the image of God. Despite the new beginning, sin continues to be a problem for human beings starting with Noah's own family. By the time the storyline reaches today's reading, humanity has joined together in an effort to reach heaven on the basis of their own power and ingenuity. What happens in this story is an echo of what took place in the Garden of Eden with Adam and Eve and the forbidden fruit. This section of Scripture is most commonly referred to as the story about the Tower of Babel.

Pray for the Spirit's Insight

Read the Passage

Understanding the Passage

What do you think is humanity's goal in building this tower?

What is God's problem with what the people are doing in today's passage?

Questions for Further Consideration

Is our world in danger of trying to be like the people of Babel today?

Related Bible Passages

Acts 2:1-11

Day 13

Scripture Reading: Genesis 12: 1-9

Creation   Covenant   Christ   Church   Conclusion

Overview: Not long ago God had flooded the world and started over with Noah and his descendents with the command, "Be fruitful and…fill the earth." In the account of the Tower of Babel humanity is found to be actively resisting this command as the Scripture records, "Come, let us build ourselves a city…so that we may make a name for ourselves and not be scattered over the face of the whole earth (Gen 11:4)." While it is difficult to pinpoint the specific reasons for God's intervention in the Babel project, the Bible does provide some important clues. Chiefly, the passage seems to indicate humanity's desire to rebel against God's direction to populate the world as the first reason for God's confusing human language. The second reason for God's intervention was that humanity was seeking to make a name for itself as opposed to praising the name of the Lord. The end result of the divine intervention in the Babel project is the fulfilling of God's commandment to Adam and Eve, and then subsequently to Noah's family, "be fruitful and multiply and fill the earth (Genesis 11:1)." Up till this point Genesis has been dealing with broad themes, such as the creation, fall, and spread of human beings across the world. Individuals have played their part but the movements have been large and taking place over many thousands of years. In today's Scripture reading the camera angle of the Bible starts to focus more sharply on the lives of individuals and their families as God's chief method for blessing the entire world and addressing the problem of sin.

Pray for the Spirit's Insight

Read the Passage

Understanding the Passage

What does God ask Abram to do in this passage?

God claims that he is going to do something through Abram. What is it?

Questions for Further Consideration

If you were Abram how would you have responded to God's message?

Related Bible Passages

Hebrews 11:8-10

DAY 14

Scripture Reading: Genesis 15 1-11

Creation   *Covenant*   Christ   Church   Conclusion

Overview: Instead of flooding the earth again or sending fire from the skies, God makes a most unexpected move in His efforts to relate to humanity by calling upon a middle easterner named Abram. This calling is not merely to let Abram know that God exists and that He desires a relationship with Abram. Rather, God asks Abram to leave his homeland, his large extended family, and to go to a foreign country that we know today as Israel. Abram is not a young man and likely had a well established and rooted life in his hometown of Ur. God's invitation to resettle in the land of Canaan is not without promise though. God is telling Abram that if he moves his family into Canaan, the entire world will be blessed through him and his descendents. This would be like if God speaking to you saying, "I'm going to literally transform the world through you. You just have to move from your hometown to a new place unknown to you or your family." In our lives God often calls us, like he did Abram, to leave the settled lives that we know, to take a risk and to live a different kind of life. Sometimes this involves changing our geographic location but it always involves moving our spiritual location. After surviving a famine in Egypt and rescuing his nephew Lot from foreign raiders, Abram finally settles in Canaan. It is here, in Abram's new homeland, that God reveals more of His purpose and plan for Abram and his family. More than merely revealing His plan to Abram God makes a formal promise, or covenant, with Abram and his descendents.

Pray for the Spirit's Insight

Read the Passage

Understanding the Passage

What is Abram's response to God's words in verse 1? Is it a fair response?

What are the contents of God's covenant with Abram?

Questions for Further Consideration

In what ways is this covenant similar to God's covenant with Noah?

Related Bible Passages

Hebrews 11:11-12

DAY 15

Scripture Reading: Genesis 15: 12-21

Creation Covenant Christ Church Conclusion

Overview: God's first words to Abram are of encouragement and hope, but Abram is now in a distant land, childless, and uncertain about his future. God reassures Abram that he will not be left childless but that he and his wife will have a son who will be the heir of their household. In Biblical times to not have children, particularly a son, was a devastating blow to a couple, often resulting in personal feelings of shame and abandonment by God. In Abram's time, child bearing was not understood to be a personal decision or enterprise. In the culture of Biblical times society valued the family and community over the individual. A person's core identity was tied to her or her family, and so a couple without children would experience social exclusion and shame as well. Yet, God's interest in blessing Abram and his wife Sarai, goes beyond giving them a child. God covenants to give Abram descendents as numerous as the stars as well as the vast expanse of land called Canaan. God responds to Abram's doubt by making a formal agreement with him. Formal treaties were often sealed by a sacrifice like the one Abram makes at God's direction. This is an amazing kind of God, who not only commands human beings, but commits Himself to keeping His own promises. In today's passage we read the rest of the story related to God's covenant with Abram and Sarah, who in the near future would be re-named by God as Abraham and Sarah respectively, to denote their status as the father and mother of many nations (Gen 17:4).

Pray for the Spirit's Insight

Read the Passage

Understanding the Passage

In Abram's dream what does God tell him about the future?

Is the land God is giving Abram unsettled or is it already inhabited?

Questions for Further Consideration

If you were Abram how would you feel about what God says in verse 13?

Related Bible Passages

Genesis 17

DAY 16

Scripture Reading: Genesis 21: 1-7

Creation   Covenant   Christ   Church   Conclusion

Overview: As the sun sets, a blazing firepot and torch pass through the prepared sacrifices symbolizing God's formal agreement to the covenant. In our world today we might understand this act as God signing on the dotted line. The agreement is now binding, not only on Abraham to be faithful in following God, but is binding upon God Himself to be loyal to Abraham. God reveals to Abraham that his descendants will inherit the land of Canaan but only after undergoing a period of slavery and darkness. While the Scripture doesn't specifically tell us how Abraham felt about this revelation, it's clear from what later happened in the Bible that Abraham and his wife Sarah weren't totally sure how God was going to pull off His promises. Desperate for a son, Sarah encourages Abraham to give birth to a son through her servant Hagar. As if to reassure this aging couple, God further covenants with Abraham in Genesis 17 in the giving of the command that all of Abraham's descendants will be circumcised as a sign of being God's people. Abraham and Sarah have a few more adventures ranging from rescuing their nephew Lot from the city of Sodom and Gomorrah to a close encounter with a local king named Abimelech. What is striking is that the Bible always communicates a high view of Abraham and his faith despite all the sins and mistakes that we find Abraham making in the book of Genesis. In today's passage God begins to fulfill His promise to Abraham by blessing Sarah with the birth of a son named Isaac.

Pray for the Spirit's Insight

Read the Passage

Understanding the Passage

What makes the birth of Isaac so amazing?

How do you think Sarah felt after giving birth to her child?

Questions for Further Consideration

Has God ever birthed something in your life that you didn't think would happen?

Related Bible Passages

Romans 9:7-9

DAY 17

Scripture Reading: Genesis 22: 1-18

Creation   Covenant   Christ   Church   Conclusion

Overview: At last, after a lifetime of shame at not having a son, Abraham and Sarah are blessed with the birth of their son Isaac. Perhaps now that they could hold the living baby in their arms, Abraham and Sarah have real hope for the rest of God's promises related to the multiplicity of their descendants and the inheritance of the land of Canaan. Sarah may now have felt justified before God and truly whole as a woman. During this time period in history the only way a woman could hope to achieve significant status was through her husband and by having children. For a lifetime Sarah may have endured doubt, ridicule from others, and a sense of God's disapproval, but now all of this was gone. Yet this happy time in Abraham and Sarah's life is not left untouched by sin. Since the Garden of Eden the propensity for human beings to separate themselves from God, from each other, and even themselves continued to manifest. You may recall that before having Isaac Sarah had encouraged her husband to take her maid Hagar as a second wife for the purpose of having children. In fact, Hagar had born a son named Ishmael to Abraham in Genesis 16. Now that Sarah has her own child by birth she turns against Hagar and sends her out into the desert where Hagar and Ishmael almost die. God intervenes and promises to bless Ishmael, whom, Muslims see as the forerunner and father of their people. Right before today's passage, Abraham makes a treaty with some of the local leaders who recognize the hand of God in his life. Everything seems to be going well for Abraham until God gives Abraham a new assignment that we read about today.

Pray for the Spirit's Insight

Read the Passage

Understanding the Passage

What is your reaction to God's command? Does it make sense to you?

Questions for Further Consideration

How did you think Isaac felt during the course of this story?

Related Bible Passages

James 2: 21-24

DAY 18

Scripture Reading: Genesis 25: 19-34

Creation   Covenant   Christ   Church   Conclusion

Overview: Many of the events in the Bible are difficult to understand and this particular story is one of them. If Abraham and Sarah were barren and without children, why did God bother to give them a son if He only intended to take him away a short time later? The Scripture makes it clear that God didn't plan to harm Isaac because God urgently tells Abraham to "not lay a hand on the boy." If Abraham had refused God's command, Isaac would not have been injured, and as we saw, even when Abraham did obey God's command Isaac remained safe and in good health. Yet, what was the purpose of God testing Abraham in what we might consider such a cruel way? It's not possible to answer this question definitively, but it does appear that God was searching Abraham's heart to see what was most important to him. In life each of us will eventually have to give everything back to God. The seasons of life and painful tragedy will take away our parents, friends, and children. God always desires that instead of wrestling to claim these people as our possessions, we hand them over to God from the very beginning. Only once we have entrusted someone to God can we truly love them. Surely this event must have loomed large in the memory of the young Isaac even as he grew older and had his own encounters with God. As the story continues Isaac grows up and marries a beautiful woman named Rebekah with whom he is truly in love. As the years pass both Abraham and Sarah die and Isaac is now the ruling patriarch and keeper of God's covenant. In today's passage we read about the struggle between Isaac's two sons, Jacob and Esau.

Pray for the Spirit's Insight

Read the Passage

Understanding the Passage

What does God tell Rebekah about the kind of men her sons will become?

What do you think of Jacob and how he treated his older brother?

Questions for Further Consideration

Have you ever felt cheated of something that was rightly yours, like Esau?

Related Bible Passages

Genesis 27:1-40

DAY 19

Scripture Reading: Genesis 37: 1-11

Creation   Covenant   Christ   Church   Conclusion

Overview: In the ancient Middle East all of the benefits, blessings, and status were given to the first son born in a family. Even though Esau and Jacob were paternal twins the rights of the first born were given to Esau because he was the first to come out of his mother's womb. Rebekah was barren, which echoes the situation of Abraham and Sarah, but God eventually opens her womb and blesses her with two sons. God informs Rebekah that her sons will be the fathers of nations, opposing nations, and that despite custom her second son, Jacob, will be the greater of the two. Throughout the Bible God continually chooses the second born son or the individual who was perceived to be the least likely person to be blessed by God. This is to emphasize that it is God who chooses and calls people to particular purposes according to His own ways and not the ways of the human world. What we know about Jacob from the Bible is that he wasn't the most moral of individuals. He deceives his brother out of his inheritance and then later in Scripture tricks his elderly father into giving him, instead of Esau, the spiritual blessing reserved for the first born (Genesis 27). Despite Jacob's sinful tendencies, God renews the covenant with him (Genesis 28:13-15) and promises to give him the same blessings He promised to Jacob's grandfather Abraham. As Genesis continues, Jacob grows up and marries two sisters named Rachel and Leah. Isaac and Rebekah pass away and with his wives Jacob gives birth to many children. Like his grandfather, Jacob is given a new name to denote God's promise to him and his descendants. Jacob is given the name Israel by God which means one who has struggled with God (Genesis 32: 28). Today's Scripture reading concerns his many sons, particularly his favorite son, Joseph.

Pray for the Spirit's Insight

Read the Passage

Understanding the Passage

What is the reaction of Joseph's family to his dream?

Questions for Further Consideration

Why was Joseph favored in a special way by his father Jacob?

Related Bible Passages

Genesis 37 26-28

DAY 20

Scripture Reading: Genesis 50: 15-21

Creation   *Covenant*   Christ   Church   Conclusion

Overview: Jacob is now advanced in years and has been blessed by God with riches material and spiritual. Jacob has several sons but he favors Joseph, born of his beloved Rachel, above all of his other sons (including his first born Reuben) and shows this by giving him a special garment. This favoritism caused Joseph's older brothers to hate him and to be hostile to the dream that seemed to indicate Joseph's future leadership of the family. God's chosen family is a motley group and decides to kill Joseph. Instead, at the suggestion of Reuben, they sell him into slavery to some Midiniate merchants who eventually sell him to a family in Egypt. From there the account of Joseph in Genesis reads like a rags to riches story. Joseph, through his God-given gift to interpret dreams, wins the favor of Pharaoh, ruler of Egypt, and becomes his second in command ruling over the nation. A famine strikes the region, including the land of Canaan where Joseph's family still lives. Thanks to his gift of dream interpretation, Joseph has been warned about this famine by God and has made all the arrangements to ensure that Egypt will have enough food to last them through the many years of unfruitful harvests. Jacob's family in the land of Canaan does not fare as well as their neighbors in Egypt. In an act of desperation Jacob sends several of his sons to Egypt to obtain food. Joseph's brothers appear before him unknowingly in an encounter that is both ironic and tragic. They do not recognize their little brother all grown up in the clothes of the ruling official. Eventually in an emotional scene, Joseph reveals himself to his brothers. Reconciliation takes place and Jacob's family is rescued from starvation. The covenant family moves to Egypt to wait out the famine and Jacob dies, which provides the background for today's passage.

Pray for the Spirit's Insight

Read the Passage

Understanding the Passage

How does Joseph respond to his brother's plea for forgiveness?

Questions for Further Consideration

Has God ever used someone's bad intentions for good in your life?

Related Bible Passages

Acts 7: 9-13

DAY 21

Scripture Reading: Exodus 1: 1-14

Creation   Covenant   Christ   Church   Conclusion

Overview: Despite Joseph's earlier grace toward his brothers they are worried that now that their father is dead Joseph will enact his vengeance on them for their cruelty so many years ago. Afraid to even speak to Joseph about their concerns, they send a desperate letter to him. Joseph is deeply moved by his brother's plea and quickly arranges to meet with them. Joseph declares his forgiveness and declares God's perspective on the events of his life, "You intended to harm me, but God intended it for good to accomplish what is now being done, the saving of many lives" (Genesis 50:19-20). Sometimes in life people or communities intend to harm us but God takes their actions and turns them around to bring blessings to our lives. This is one of the principal themes of Scripture and the Christian life. Namely, that God can take the unfortunate circumstances and pains of life and birth transformation and blessings through them. The brothers had no idea that God was using them, and until many years later Joseph didn't have this global perspective either. Sometimes we need to pause in the midst of our troubles and climb up a tree to see God's global perspective on our situation. The book of Genesis concludes with the death of Joseph, and then beginning in Exodus we learn about the fate of Joseph's descendents in Egypt.

Pray for the Spirit's Insight

Read the Passage

Understanding the Passage

Do you hear any echoes of the book of Genesis in verses 6-7?

What does it mean that "a new king, who did not know about Joseph, came to power in Egypt?"

Questions for Further Consideration

Clearly the Israelites remained in Egypt well beyond the famine during the time of Joseph and his brothers. Was it God's intention for them to settle in Egypt?

Related Bible Passages

Psalm 105: 8-25

DAY 22

Scripture Reading: Exodus 2: 1-10

Creation   Covenant   Christ   Church   Conclusion

Overview: The descendants of Jacob and Joseph have apparently settled in Egypt where God's covenant blessing to be fruitful and multiply (Genesis 1:28) has been realized. It seems unlikely that such a remarkable figure as Joseph would have been completely forgotten by Pharaoh or the wider Egyptian culture in a literal sense. It may be that over the centuries the role of Joseph was down played by the Egyptians or that the new Pharaoh had a personal prejudice against the Jewish people. It is evident that the new king felt threatened, perhaps even legitimately so, by the prosperity and growing population of the Hebrew people. Whatever the reason, the covenant people of the One God are enslaved in the land that had formerly been a refuge for them. Of course, God's intention was never that the Israelites settle in Israel for He had given them the land of Canaan as an everlasting inheritance (Genesis 17:8). The Pharaoh's fear results in an edict of unimagined barbarity when he orders that every Hebrew boy that is born must be thrown into the Nile (Exodus 1:22) in order to die. Born into this time of tragedy is a Jewish boy named Moses. From the moment of the child's birth Moses' parents must have been concerned for the safety of their son. Moses is regarded as the greatest figure in the pages of Old Testament and continues to be revered by Jews and Christians around the world as a model of faithfulness. Today's passage gives us insight into the beginning of Moses' life.

Pray for the Spirit's Insight

Read the Passage

Understanding the Passage

How do you think Moses' mother felt when she put her son in the Nile?

Do you think God was working in some of the convenient details of this story?

Questions for Further Consideration

Does Moses have any siblings? How do you know?

Related Bible Passages

Acts 7: 20-22

DAY 23

Scripture Reading: Exodus 3:1-10

Creation   Covenant   Christ   Church   Conclusion

Overview: A nation has embraced sin in the form of slavery and infant murder. Moses' mother must have felt stuck between a rock and a hard place. She knew that it would be impossible to keep Moses hidden from the Egyptian authorities as he got older. If discovered, he would be killed. She likely felt a mixture of guilt, desperation, and hope as she pushed her baby out onto the Nile River. Whether or not Moses' mother and sister knew that the king's daughter frequented this part of the river is unknown. However, the fact that the princess responded in a favorable way to the baby and was so open to the suggestion of a slave girl speaks to the way that God works in the everyday details of life. Moses goes on to live with his adopted mother in the affluence of the Princess' palace. There is some evidence from the Scriptures that Moses stayed in touch with his Hebrew roots while also being raised in the royal society and culture of the Egyptians. On one occasion Moses sees an Egyptian beating several Hebrew slaves. His reaction is to take immediate action by killing the Egyptian. Initially, Moses believed that the incident with the Egyptian was a secret, done in private, and unknown to the public. Shortly after the incident takes place, he learns that his actions are widely known within the Hebrew community and potentially beyond. Fearing retribution from his adopted family and culture he flees to the land of Midian. There he becomes a shepherd, marries, and builds a life for himself far away from his former lifestyle as a prince of Egypt. Today's reading concerns Moses' call from God to leave Midian, and eventually Egypt, forever.

Pray for the Spirit's Insight

Read the Passage

Understanding the Passage

How does God reveal Himself to Moses?

How does God communicate to Moses that He is the God of Moses' people

Questions for Further Consideration

What burning bushes have you experienced in your own life?

Related Bible Passages
Acts 7: 30-34

DAY 24

Scripture Reading: Exodus 3: 11-20

Creation   Covenant   Christ   Church   Conclusion

Overview: Moses has long since left Egypt and his own Hebrew people who lived as slaves in the land of the Nile. Moses is now living among another foreign people as a shepherd for his father-in-law, Jethro. As a shepherd Moses would have spent years leading sheep through the often treacherous and barren landscapes of the Middle East. This experience of being a shepherd no doubt prepared Moses for the future task that God was giving him to lead the Hebrew people to freedom. Moses is deep within the wilderness near the Mountain of Sinai, which is considered an especially holy place all throughout the Bible, when God reveals Himself to Moses in the form of a burning bush. To encounter God in the Old Testament was to experience an overwhelming sense of awe, majesty, and respectful fear. Befitting such an encounter Moses seeks to conceal his face as God speaks to him from the burning bush. This is holy ground because God is revealing Himself to one of His children, made in His image. The burning bushes that we encounter in our own lives are not usually as obvious and supernatural as the one we read about in Exodus. Nevertheless, God enters into the ordinary experience of our lives by creating spiritual fires that grab our attention. These spiritual fires can be almost anything, ranging from a personal experience of suffering to a job transition that changes how you look at the world or understand yourself. The God of Abraham, Isaac, and Jacob has revealed Himself to Moses and assigned him a divine mission of liberation. In today's passage we read about Moses' reaction to this high calling.

Pray for the Spirit's Insight

Read the Passage

Understanding the Passage

Moses isn't sure he is qualified for this assignment. Can you relate to his doubt?

What do you think of the name God gives Himself in verse 14?

Questions for Further Consideration

Do you have any idea of what God's calling in your life is?

Related Bible Passages

John 8:58

DAY 25

Scripture Reading: Exodus 7: 14-24

Creation   Covenant   Christ   Church   Conclusion

Overview: People often remark that if they could be sure God was speaking to them they would do whatever God directed. Moses, considered the greatest figure in the Old Testament, is excellent proof that certainty in hearing God does not always lead to immediate obedience on the part of human beings. In the burning bush encounter Moses essentially tells God, "Please choose someone else, I'm not qualified." In many cases when God speaks to us we are not excited about the experience because God is calling us to do something that we would rather not do. Like Moses, we often balk at the idea of God using us to bless someone else in a significant way. In religious circles people often make the mistake of assuming that it is the spiritual leader's job to do God's work and theirs is to watch him or her do it. It is every single believer's job to do God's work in the time and place they find themselves. While theological training, life experience, and natural gifts are helpful none are needed except God's call. The God that appeared to Moses is named, " I AM," to signify God's eternal being, presence, and undeniable reality. God enlists Aaron, a gifted speaker, to serve as the spokesperson for his brother Moses. Moses and Aaron then proceed to begin their mission of liberation by speaking to Pharaoh and the Hebrew people. In today's passage God seeks to bring glory to Himself and freedom to His people by unleashing the first of many plagues against Egypt.

Pray for the Spirit's Insight

Read the Passage

Understanding the Passage

According to the passage what has been Pharaoh's reaction to Moses' requests?

After the first plague, the plague of blood, does Pharaoh change his mind?

Questions for Further Consideration

Can you identify with Pharaoh's unyielding heart and stubbornness?

Related Bible Passages

Romans 9:17

DAY 26

Scripture Reading: Exodus 12: 1-14

Creation   Covenant   Christ   Church   Conclusion

Overview: Pharaoh is the ruler of a powerful nation with an assortment of powerful gods and goddesses and seems unmoved by the supernatural threats that God works through Moses and Aaron. The Egyptian court magicians were able to duplicate some of the miracles wrought by Moses and Aaron, such as turning water into blood. Whether this was done by trickery or through the use of dark supernatural powers, we cannot be certain. The first plague of blood, which attacked the source of life for Egyptian civilization, the Nile, did not result in Pharaoh changing his mind. In fact, after the plague of blood God continues to work supernatural events through Moses and Aaron bringing a total of nine more plagues. A pattern is established from the very first plague of blood. God orders Moses and Aaron to go to Pharaoh and demand the freedom of their people. They are to warn Pharaoh that another plague will come if he refuses to let the Hebrews go. In every instance Pharaoh ultimately refuses to let the Hebrews go into the desert to worship their God. This refusal on Pharaoh's part is impressive in the sense that his kingdom is being devastated by these divine plagues which his own gods seem powerless to stop. This divine competition between the pagan gods of Egypt (which included Pharaoh himself) and the Hebrew's God proves the existence of one God and one God alone: the God of Abraham, Isaac, and Jacob. In today's passage we read about the establishment of the celebration of Passover and its relationship to the last plague of the firstborn.

Pray for the Spirit's Insight

Read the Passage

Understanding the Passage

What does the Lord command the Israelites to do?

What is the relationship between the Passover and the plague of the firstborn?

Questions for Further Consideration

Has God ever arranged a "Passover" in your own life?

Related Bible Passages

Matthew 26:2

DAY 27

Scripture Reading: Exodus 14: 21-31

Creation   Covenant   Christ   Church   Conclusion

Overview: The plague of the firstborn was the final blow that initially broke Pharaoh's hardened heart. Every Egyptian, whether prince or pauper, lost a family member during this plague. Finally, Pharaoh relents, and gives permission to Moses and Aaron for their people to go out and worship their God. According to the Scriptures, the Egyptians encouraged the Hebrews to leave as quickly as possible even providing them with food and jewelry (Exodus 12:33). Many Egyptians believed that if the Hebrews didn't leave, they would all die at the hands of the Hebrews' God. The celebration of the Passover meal was established by God to protect the Israelites from the plague of the firstborn. Any Jewish house which had blood on the door would literally be passed-over by the plague. In addition, it was during this time that God established the practice of consecrating every firstborn male, human or animal, from that time on, to God. In the future and until this present day the principal focus of the Passover celebration is the liberation of the Israelites from slavery in Egypt. Once Pharaoh gave permission for the Israelites to leave they began their journey toward the desert. However, Pharaoh shortly thereafter changed his mind and assembled his army to catch up to the Hebrews. In today's passage we read about the famous crossing of the sea and the final chapter in the Exodus event from Egypt.

Pray for the Spirit's Insight

Read the Passage

Understanding the Passage

How does God, through Moses, part the Sea?

What happens to the Egyptian army that is pursuing the Israelites?

Questions for Further Consideration

How do you think the Israelites felt after witnessing these events?

Related Bible Passages

1 Corinthians 10:2

DAY 28

Scripture Reading: Exodus 19: 1-9

Creation   Covenant   Christ   Church   Conclusion

Overview: When the Israelites realized that the Egyptian army was pursuing them, they must have felt anxious, fearful, and uncertain about the success of their journey. While the Hebrews were numerous, they were not armed or trained in the ways of war like the Egyptian army. If they had not been pursued, the Israelites could have simply walked around the sea that now formed a deadly obstacle before them. However, the God that had worked deadly wonders in the plagues worked a miracle of salvation by parting the sea with powerful winds. The Hebrews passed through the waters on dry land to the other side. At God's command Moses stretched out his hand and the waters returned washing away the Egyptian army, ending all of their lives. The Hebrews must have felt relieved, inspired, and in awe of this God that had set them free from their chains. These were not events that the Hebrew people would forget easily as they entered the desert to make their way to the land promised to their ancestors, Abraham, Isaac, and Jacob. Interestingly, it does not take long for the Israelites to complain about their new situation. They desire water (Exodus 15:25), and they demand food (Exodus 16) which God provides through miraculous means. As they travel they arrive at Sinai were Moses ascends the mountain for a special encounter with God. In today's passage we read about this encounter and the offer God makes to Moses and his people.

Pray for the Spirit's Insight

Read the Passage

Understanding the Passage

What does God offer Moses and his people?

Do you hear any echoes of the book of Genesis in this passage?

Questions for Further Consideration

Are the people interested in God's offer?

Related Bible Passages

Acts 7:38

DAY 29

Scripture Reading: Exodus 20: 1-11

Creation   Covenant   Christ   Church   Conclusion

Overview: After rescuing the Israelites from slavery in Egypt, God seeks to restore the covenant he made with Abraham, Isaac, and Jacob with the whole nation of Israel. When the Lord speaks to Moses on the holy mountain the words echo earlier encounters between God and the patriarchs (Abraham, Isaac, and Jacob). God promises to continue the covenant He first made with Abraham with the nation of Israel. The covenant involves not only God's promise to be faithful to Israel but for the people to be exclusively faithful to the One God. When Moses describes the terms of the covenant to the Israelites, they are eager to accept God's promises and pledge themselves to "do everything the Lord has said." Then following God's instructions, Moses tells the people to prepare themselves for God's special visitation three days later. In the Old Testament to encounter God was to encounter a being that is pure, powerful, and totally unlike humanity. Preparation for an encounter with God often involved ritual cleaning and abstinence from sexual relations. The covenant people prepare themselves according to Moses' instructions and await God's revelation on the mountaintop. It is here on Mt. Sinai that God reveals the holy way of life that the Israelites are to live by. It is more than a mere listing of laws, though it takes that form, it is the first explicit giving of God's Word to God's people. In today's reading we learn about the contents of this special message.

Pray for the Spirit's Insight

Read the Passage

Understanding the Passage

How are the Israelites to relate to idols according to this passage?

How is the commandment to keep Sabbath rooted in the book of Genesis?

Questions for Further Consideration

Which of these first four commandments do you struggle with?

Of these commandments which one do you think is least observed today?

Related Bible Passages

Deuteronomy 5:4-15

DAY 30

Scripture Reading: Exodus 20: 12-21

Creation   Covenant   Christ   Church   Conclusion

Overview: In the first four commandments God addresses the essential aspects of human life. First, humans beings are commanded to put God before all else, and second, to recognize the finitude of life and the need for rest and restoration. God alone is infinite and all-powerful while humans being must keep Sabbath to maintain their physical and spiritual health. Sabbath keeping is an essential aspect of Biblical spirituality and is rooted in the creation story where God Himself rested on the seventh day (Genesis 2:2). The cyclical pattern of resting and activity can be found in nature and is evident in the lives of God's people throughout the Scriptures. The worship of idols, statues, and symbols of pagan deities was a common practice during the time of the Exodus. The Ten Commandments were very clear in stating that the Israelites were forbidden to make, reverence, or worship idols. Furthermore, God indicates that the consequences for worshipping idols will extend beyond the offender to his or her descendants. The Ten Commandments are part of the covenant promise that Israel makes with God. The Lord has promised to be Israel's God, but the Israelites in turn have promised to be His people. The Ten Commandments have had an enormous influence, not only in the Jewish and Christian faiths, but also on the ideals of justice and morality throughout Western Civilization. In today's passage we read about the remaining six commandments that God gave the people of Israel from Mt. Sinai.

Pray for the Spirit's Insight

Read the Passage

Understanding the Passage

What is the promise to those who honor their father and mother?

Is it against the commandments to kill someone?

Questions for Further Consideration

Which of these six commandments do you struggle with the most?

Of these commandments which one do you think is least observed today?

Related Bible Passages

Deuteronomy 5:16-22

DAY 31

Scripture Reading: Exodus 32: 1-11

Creation   Covenant   Christ   Church   Conclusion

Overview: In the remaining six commandments God gives instruction to the Israelites regarding the proper way for human beings to treat one another. What is striking about the Ten Commandments is that they are given for all of the Jewish people. Often in ancient cultures there would be one set of laws for the elite and another set of laws for the common people. Interestingly, the commandment to honor parents carries with it a promise that "you may live long in the land the LORD your God is giving you (Exodus 20:12)." Honoring parents encompassed not only showing respect, but also included supporting aging parents financially. Also tied to the commandment of honoring parents is an implicit charge to honor the beliefs one's ancestors who could be traced back to Abraham. The word used in the sixth commandment is best-translated "murder" and not simply "kill". People of faith have long struggled to discern if there is ever a time where it would be considered a God anointed act to kill someone. Regardless of one's perspective on the use of force, it can be agreed that violence was not a part of God's original plan for humanity in the Garden of Eden. It was not until sin entered the world that the first murder took place when Cain slew his brother Abel (Genesis 4). After receiving the Ten Commandments Moses goes back up into the cloud of presence to receive from God further details related to the life of the covenant people. These instructions would later be codified and referred to as the Law of Moses. In today's passage we read about the people's reaction as Moses is delayed in coming down from the mountain.

Pray for the Spirit's Insight

Read the Passage

Understanding the Passage

What commandments do God's people violate in this passage?

What is God's reaction to the people's worship of the Golden Calf?

Questions for Further Consideration

Why do you think the people quickly forget the God that had set them free?

Related Bible Passages

Psalm 106: 19-21

DAY 32

Scripture Reading: Exodus 32: 15-24

Creation   Covenant   Christ   Church   Conclusion

Overview: God reveals Himself with magnificence from the mountaintop, and no sooner has He given the Ten Commandments to the covenant people, than they break the most important commandment of all, "You shall have no other gods before me" (Exodus 20:4). God's reaction is passionate, echoing the anger of a person who has been betrayed by a person he loves. Moses intercedes on behalf of God's people, and it appears that God will continue to be faithful to the covenant He established with Israel. It is difficult to fathom how the chosen people could so quickly forget the God who worked miracles to set them free in Egypt. Perhaps more astonishing is that the person who leads the people in this idolatry is no unknown rebel but Moses' own brother, Aaron. Yet, if we consider the story of God throughout the pages of the Bible thus far this situation is not all that surprising. Even within paradise Adam and Eve chose their own way over God's way causing a permanent rift between the will of human beings and the will of God (Genesis 3). God's giving of the Ten Commandants, and the rest of the Law, was intended to provide a holy way of life that His people could follow which would keep them in connection with God. The commandments were intended to be more than rules of good behavior, but were given as a means of nurturing and preserving relationships between God and people. In today's reading Moses descends from the mountaintop and confronts his brother Aaron about what has happened.

Pray for the Spirit's Insight

Read the Passage

Understanding the Passage

What is Moses' reaction when he sees the Israelites dancing around the golden calf?

What is Aaron's excuse for leading the people in idolatry?

Questions for Further Consideration

If you were an Israelite, do you think you would have protested the idol worship?

Related Bible Passages

Genesis 3: 11-13

DAY 33

Scripture Reading: Deuteronomy 6: 1-12

Creation   Covenant   Christ   Church   Conclusion

Overview: Moses descends from the mountain and is filled with anger over the idolatrous actions of his people. It is interesting that Moses' emotions echo the expressed emotions of God in the previous passage (Exodus 32:10). In his rage Moses smashes the tablets containing the Ten Commandments at the foot of the mountain. He has the golden calf melted down into particles, scatters the particles in water, and forces the people to drink it. Aaron then mumbles his way through an excuse about the people being impatient with Moses' delay and claims that the golden calf mysteriously leaped out of the fire by itself. Aaron's reply to his brother Moses is a screaming echo of a conversation that took place in the Garden of Eden in which Adam and Eve did everything to blame somebody else but did not take personal responsibility for their own actions (Genesis 3:12-13). After this, Moses administers punishment to the people of Israel and returns to the mountaintop to receive a second copy of the Law. Israel then continues through the desert toward the Promised Land under God's protection. More details are established relating to the proper worship of God, the establishment of the Tent of Meeting (the place where God would descend in a cloud and speak to Moses), as well as the Hebrew priesthood and the related need for animal sacrifices (see the book of Leviticus). Facing many trials, the people of Israel finally (after 2 generations of wandering) arrived at the banks of the Jordan River. In today's passage Moses challenges God's people to be faithful to the commandments as they prepare to enter the Promised Land.

Pray for the Spirit's Insight

Read the Passage

Understanding the Passage

How are the Israelites instructed to love God?

Does the passage give evidence of people's living in the Promised Land?

Questions for Further Consideration

Which commandments or instructions in these passage do you observe?

Related Bible Passages

Mark 12:28-30

DAY 34

Scripture Reading: Deuteronomy 34: 1-12

Creation   Covenant   Christ   Church   Conclusion

Overview: The covenant people are instructed to love God with "all your heart, and with all your soul, and with all your strength (Deut. 6:5)." This is the very heart of the Old Testament Law; not that people would merely obey rules and regulations, but that their entire life would be rooted in the love of God. While the first five books of the Bible, often referred to as the Torah, are filled with numerous laws (613 laws by traditional reckoning!) the purpose of these requirements was to establish a way of life that allowed people to live in union with God and with each other. The sacrifices required by the Law of Moses (see Leviticus 1-5) were meant to be understood as sacred rituals which led to reconciliation between people and God, not as payments of appeasement to an angry God. Even today people of faith can fall into the trap of viewing their participation in worship and spiritual practices as payment for divine favors. We must strive to not fall into this trap but to understand our worship and spiritual practices as ways of nurturing our relationship with God. Across the Jordan River in the land of Canaan is a land flowing with milk and honey, but it is also a land filled with numerous groups of people. This is indicated by God's promise that the people of Israel will enjoy houses, cities, and fields that they did not build or labor to establish (Deut. 6:10-11). This will present a considerable challenge to God's people as they attempt to claim the land promised to their ancestors, Abraham, Isaac, and Jacob. In today's passage we read about Moses' death just prior to the Israelites entry into the land of Canaan.

Pray for the Spirit's Insight

Read the Passage

Understanding the Passage

What does God show Moses on top of Mount Nebo?

When Moses' dies are the Israelites left leaderless?

Questions for Further Consideration

How do you think Moses' felt realizing he would not make it into the promised land?

Related Bible Passages

Matthew 17: 1-13

DAY 35

Scripture Reading: Joshua 5:13 - Joshua 6:1-5

Creation   Covenant   Christ   Church   Conclusion

Overview: After decades of dedication and struggle to liberate his people, Moses ascends the Mount of Nebo. Here the Lord shows him all of the land that the Israelites will possess, including some of the tribal boundaries that will be established. While the twelve tribes of Israel will enter and take possession of the land of Canaan, as promised to their forefather Abraham, Moses himself will die before setting foot in the promised land. We don't know how Moses' felt about this situation except to guess that he may have felt a mixture of anger, and disappointment, as well as relief that his task was now over. Without doubt Moses is the greatest figure of the Old Testament, walking in a close and personal relationship with God. Yet, upon Moses' death, the people of Israel are not left without a leader. Joshua who served as Moses' assistant since his youth, takes the mantle of leadership from his mentor and proceeds to lead the Israelites across the Jordan River. God commands Joshua to conquer the land and claim the inheritance that is rightfully the possession of God's people. Once Israel crosses the Jordan Israelite spies quickly come into contact with foreign people and cities. Various tribal nations with their own gods and customs already dwell in the land of Canaan. The presence of these foreign people, who do not believe in the one God of Israel, will prove to be a stumbling block for God's chosen people for years. In today's reading Joshua is directed by God to take the city of Jericho through a divinely crafted strategy.

Pray for the Spirit's Insight

Read the Passage

Understanding the Passage

Do you hear any echoes of the book of Exodus in this passage?

Who delivers the message regarding Jericho to Joshua?

Questions for Further Consideration

If you were an aide to Joshua what would you think of the battle strategy for Jericho?

Related Bible Passages

Hebrews 11:30

DAY 36

Scripture Reading: Judges 7: 1-6

Creation   Covenant   Christ   Church   Conclusion

Overview: Jericho was well fortified and word had spread of the coming attack by the Israelites. An angel of the Lord then visits Moses' successor, Joshua. In a scene that echoes Moses' encounter with God in the burning bush, Joshua is instructed to, "take off your sandals, for the place where you are standing is holy (Joshua 5:15)." The angel informs Joshua that He will give victory to the Israel if they obey God's instructions. God's plan involves carrying the Ark of the Covenant in procession around the city for six days. On the seventh day the priests are to process seven times around the city, trumpets are to be blown, and all of the people of Israel are to shout, which God promises will cause the walls of Jericho to tumble down. The Ark of the Covenant (see Exodus 25:10-22) was believed to contain the presence of the Lord and symbolized His throne on earth. In faith, Joshua and his people carry out the Lord's plan, and on the seventh day the walls of Jericho collapse. In this battle, as in many battles in the Old Testament, the Bible stresses the role of God in obtaining the victory for the people as opposed to the Israelites claiming victory for themselves. Over several years Joshua leads his people to more victories, and they eventually conquer the Promised Land. The conquest is not totally complete and future leaders of Israel, who were called judges, would each have to fight wars with foreign peoples. The judges were more like military leaders than our understanding of modern day judges. Some ruled over all of Israel while some ruled over parts of Israel. In today's passage, years after Joshua, we read about Gideon, a judge of Israel, who attempts to defeat one of his nations' enemies, the Midianites.

Pray for the Spirit's Insight

Read the Passage

Understanding the Passage

Is God satisfied with the number of men in Gideon's Army?

What is the method God uses to downsize the Army?

Questions for Further Consideration

In verse 3 many abandon the army, what might this tell you about the situation?

Related Bible Passages

Judges 6

DAY 37

Scripture Reading: Judges 7: 9-24

Creation   Covenant   Christ   Church   Conclusion

Overview: From the selected passages we don't know a lot about the kind of person Gideon was. However, other portions of Scripture paint Gideon as a cautious fellow, who, like his ancestor Moses, questions the message of the Lord (Judges 1:11-17). However, Gideon's character is stellar in comparison to many of the judges who ruled over Israel. As a group they were a motley lot that included a left-handed man (Ehud, Judges 3:15), a woman (Deborah, Judges 4:4), and a man with super strength whose sexual mores were deplorable (Samson, Judges 16:1), but God chose to use each of them anyway. In fact, the reason that God is not satisfied with the size of Gideon's army is the same reason that God often uses terribly imperfect people in the Bible and in our world today to carry out His purposes. That reason is to make it clear that without God the imperfect person or Gideon's army would not have been able to succeed. This is the regular pattern that God establishes in the Old Testament and continues to build upon through the whole story of God from the beginning of the New Testament to the end of the Bible in the book of Revelation. Interestingly, the passage tell us that twenty-two thousand men left the army when given the opportunity (Judges 7:3). This may tell us about the severity of the situation that most people perceived in the threat coming from the Midianites. In a potentially dire situation, God does not add to the number of the army but reduces its numbers by selecting only the men who lapped the water while drinking. In today's passage we read about Gideon's attack with his three hundred men against the Midian camp.

Pray for the Spirit's Insight

Read the Passage

Understanding the Passage

God gives Gideon some assurance of his victory over the Midianites; how so?

Gideon devises a battle strategy of his own in attacking the camp; what is it?

Questions for Further Consideration

According to the passage why do the Midianites attack each other?

Related Bible Passages

Hebrews 11:32

DAY 38

Scripture Reading: 1 Samuel 1: 1-11

Creation   Covenant   Christ   Church   Conclusion

Overview: Gideon is a cautious fellow who never is assured by his divine encounters with God. God has promised to defeat the Midianites with Gideon's small army of three hundred. Gideon must have had some reservations about this plan because the Lord reassures Gideon of the battle's success by having him eavesdrop on a dream of one the Midian soldiers. Yet, Gideon still devises his own plan in carrying out the attack by dividing his men into three companies. Gideon orders all of the men to carry jars with torches inside, as well as a trumpet, which they were to blow when he gave the signal. The success of the attack is immediately evident, and the enemy army, under divine influence, even began to attack each other before retreating. Gideon's army pursues the Midianites across the countryside to victory not only in this battle, but for the entire war against Midian. After Gideon's victory Israel enjoys a period of peace before the next threat emerges calling for a new military leader to protect Israel. This is the essential pattern in the Book of Judges; a threat emerges against Israel, a judge is raised up, peace follows, and then the cycle begins again. Israel, unlike the nations surrounding it did not have a human king because God was to be Israel's only sovereign. One of the ways that God communicated His purposes to Israel during the time of the judges, and later on in Scripture, was through prophets and seers. These men were given a special ability to hear and proclaim the voice of God. In today's passage we read about the mother of the last judge of Israel who was also a gifted prophet and priest of God.

Pray for the Spirit's Insight

Read the Passage

Understanding the Passage

Does Elkanah despise his wife Hannah because she has given him no children?

What does Hannah promise God if He grants her a child?

Questions for Further Consideration

What do you think life was like for Hannah on a regular basis?

Related Bible Passages

Exodus 23: 14-19

DAY 39

Scripture Reading: 1 Samuel 3: 1-21

Creation   Covenant   Christ   Church   Conclusion

Overview: The situation that Elkanah and Hannah find themselves in is not a new one. We can find echoes of their situation in the stories of Abraham and Sarah (Gen. 21), Isaac and Rebekah (Gen.25:21), and Jacob and Rachel (Gen. 29:31). Though Elkanah's other wife Penninnah had given birth to children he clearly loved Hannah more. In the ancient Middle East there were no opportunities for a woman to establish herself as a person of worth to society except by marrying and having children. Daily life must have been rough for Hannah, especially since Penninnah was apparently given to ridiculing her. The love of her husband may have made the situation somewhat bearable, but at best the rest of the community in which she lived would have pitied her. Hannah, in an act of desperation and hope, prays a passionate prayer at the temple that she would conceive a son. She promises that if the Lord grants her request she will dedicate the boy to the Lord's service. As time passes it becomes evident that the Lord has heard her prayer. At last she must have felt blessed by God, worthy of her husband's love, and vindicated in the eyes of those who condemned her. After weaning the boy, she brings him to the priest Eli, who along with his two sons, rules over Israel and presides at the religious services of the temple. Eli is an old man, with a kind heart and a dedication to the Lord, but his sons are out of control. They are stealing the best meat from the sacrifices, sleeping with the servant girls, and in general disrespecting God. The boy Samuel lives with the priestly family and learns the way of the Lord from Eli. In today's reading we learn about Samuel's first divine encounter with the Lord.

Pray for the Spirit's Insight

Read the Passage

Understanding the Passage

How does Samuel know that it is God speaking to him?

What message does the Lord give to the boy Samuel?

Questions for Further Consideration

What do you think of Eli's reaction to Samuel's news from God in verse 18?

Related Bible Passages

Genesis 22:11

DAY 40

Scripture Reading: 1 Samuel 8: 1-9

Creation   Covenant   Christ   Church   Conclusion

Overview: In the quiet of the night, the boy Samuel hears a voice calling for him. He assumes that it is Eli, his foster father and mentor, and so he gets up and goes to him. Eli assures Samuel that he didn't call for him and that he should go back to bed. At Samuel's third insistence that he heard a voice, Eli makes the connection that the Lord is speaking to the boy. In our own journeys of faith we need to have our own mentors, who may not be old chronologically like Eli, but who are old in the faith and can help us discern when God is really speaking to us. The message that God reveals to Samuel is that the days of the House of Eli are limited and that Eli and his sons will soon face the consequences for their transgressions against the Lord. The basic unit of the human population was not the individual in Biblical times (nor in many cultures today) but the family. The actions of some members of the family were seen to be the actions of the entire family, especially in this case, since it was Eli's responsibility to discipline his sons, which he failed to do. Eli's reaction is a startling one showing no anger toward Samuel, no regret over his parenting style, or a sudden desire to punish his two adult children. It's hard to know exactly what motivated Eli to respond in this way, whether it was a desire that the Lord's will be done or that, like with his sons, he wasn't going to object to anything but simply roll with the punches of life. In the coming years the prophecy regarding Eli and his sons comes to pass resulting in all of their deaths. Samuel becomes the judge, priest, and prophet of Israel ruling with justice and righteous for many long years. In today's passage we read about the people of Israel and Samuel in his old age.

Pray for the Spirit's Insight

Read the Passage

Understanding the Passage

Why don't the elders of Israel want Samuel's sons to rule as judges?

Samuel feels rejected by his own people, but what does God's tell him?

Questions for Further Consideration

Do you think you have ever been rejected because someone was rejecting God?

Related Bible Passages

Deuteronomy 17: 14-20

DAY 41

Scripture Reading: 1 Samuel 10: 17-26

Creation   Covenant   Christ   Church   Conclusion

Overview: Samuel, after a lifetime of faithfully serving God and ruling Israel, finds himself in an ironic situation. While he appoints his sons, Joel and Abijah, to be his successors in ruling Israel, the people will not have it. Apparently, Samuel's sons, like Eli's sons before him, are not faithful priests and are committed to using their position of power for their own gain and not for the benefit of others. The elders of the people voice the desire of the whole nation in asking for a king. From the people's perspective a king would provide a stable leadership structure, as well as demonstrate to the surrounding nations that Israel is just like them, and just as progressive. Samuel feels rejected, perhaps insulted, by this request but God tells Samuel, "it is not you they have rejected, but they have rejected me as their king" (1 Samuel 8:7). God goes on to say that this has been the pattern of Israel's behavior ever since He led them out of slavery and bondage in Egypt. For believers in the Old Testament, up to the present time, the constant question of spiritual health is whether or not we have replaced the king of our lives, God, with someone or something else. There have been hints in the Bible up to this point that one day Israel would have a king (see Deut. 17:14 for example) but it does not begin to manifest as a reality until the people make this request of Samuel. So God relents and tells the people through Samuel that they will have a king along with the negative consequences of human rule. God directs Samuel to anoint Saul, the son of Kish, a young man of the tribe of Benjamin as Israel's first king. In today's passage we read about the public installation of Saul as King of Israel.

Pray for the Spirit's Insight

Read the Passage

Understanding the Passage

Before installing Saul as King what message from the Lord does Samuel deliver?

Does Saul appear eager to accept the kingship of Israel?

Questions for Further Consideration

Are all the people of Israel excited about Saul being the new king?

Related Bible Passages

1 Samuel 9:18-27, 10:1-8

DAY 42

Scripture Reading: 1 Samuel 13: 1-15

Creation   Covenant   Christ   Church   Conclusion

Overview: Before declaring Saul as king Samuel informs Israel that they have rejected the God of their ancestors. The rejection lies in their desire to a have a human king over the divine kingship of the Lord. God grants the people's request for a king and will use the monarchy to carry out His great purposes in history. Saul is from a small family of the tribe of Benjamin but is God's choice to be the first monarch of Israel. As each tribe, clan, and family was selected, the thousands of people assembled must have felt a great sense of anticipation about who would be their king. Some of the more prominent men no doubt felt they were going to be selected. Imagine how you would have felt hearing the announcement of the new king's name. Then imagine your reaction when you heard someone say that the man declared to be your new king was hiding with the baggage! Nevertheless, Saul is pulled to the center of the crowd and is announced as king over Israel. Many rejoiced at this announcement but some seemed to have no use for Saul. Perhaps this is because Israel still faced many enemies and they wondered what kind of warrior the new king would be after finding him hiding in the luggage? However, in the future Saul proves himself by winning a military victory over the Ammonites. Israel continued to have many enemies from the nations inhabiting and surrounding the promiseland. For Saul, his chief concern was to establish security and national boundaries for the country. In today's passage we read about how Saul oversteps his authority as king and is rejected by God.

Pray for the Spirit's Insight

Read the Passage

Understanding the Passage

What does Saul do that results in God rejecting him as king?

What is Saul's explanation or excuse to Samuel for what he did?

Questions for Further Consideration

Do you think God's punishment of Samuel is fair?

Related Bible Passages

1 Samuel 12:12-15

DAY 43

Scripture Reading: 1 Samuel 16: 1-13

Creation   Covenant   Christ   Church   Conclusion

Overview: In the Old Testament it was commanded in the Law that only priests could offer the appointed sacrifices (see Leviticus 1:1-9). The Hebrew priesthood was hereditary; that is you had to be a descendant of Moses' brother, Aaron, in order to be a priest. The priests presided at the services at the temple. No one else was allowed to perform these sacred rights. One of the jobs of the king of Israel was to uphold the teachings of the law. Saul, feeling pressured by the military situation and Samuel's delay decides to offer the religious sacrifices himself. No sooner has Saul done this then Samuel arrives outraged at what the king has done. Samuel explains that because Saul believed he could violate the Law without penalty, the Lord has rejected him as Israel's king. In fact, Samuel explains that God has chosen another man, one who is close to God's heart, to become his replacement. However, this replacement does not happen right away. While Samuel is aware of God's will in this matter, the rest of Israel is not. Saul, along with this son Jonathan, continues to live and rule as the chief royalty of the nation. Saul seeks to make no amends for his actions related to offering the sacrifices, and in fact, violates another command of God in a later battle, solidifying his rejection by God. Samuel's warning to the people regarding the pitfalls of human kingship is already coming to pass in Saul. However, the reign of Saul does not come to an end even when God's new choice for king is obvious to many people in Israel. In today's passage we read about Samuel's anointing of an unlikely candidate who will not only become Israel's next king, but next to Moses perhaps the greatest figure in all of Israel's history.

Pray for the Spirit's Insight

Read the Passage

Understanding the Passage

Are there any indications that Saul is trying to control Samuel in this passage?

Why is David such an unlikely choice to be the next king of Israel?

Questions for Further Consideration

What does verse 7 tell us about God's perspective on humanity?

Related Bible Passages

Psalm 78: 70-72

DAY 44

Scripture Reading: 1 Samuel 17: 32-51

Creation   Covenant   Christ   Church   Conclusion

Overview: Saul has violated the commandment of the Lord and has been rejected as Israel's king by God. God commands Samuel to go to Bethlehem, so that he can anoint one of Jesse's sons as the new king. Samuel is impressed by the eldest son Eliab and initially believes that he has found Israel's new king. However, God reveals to Samuel that He has not chosen Eliab or any of Jesse's other sons that are present. In verse 7 God tells Samuel, "The Lord does not look at the things man looks at. Man looks at the outward appearance, but the Lord looks at the heart." All through the history of the Bible God has often raised up people who seemed like unlikely candidates for leadership. In ancient times, if anyone was going to become powerful or significant in a family, it would be the eldest son. He inherited a double portion of his father's wealth and his father's blessing of spiritual leadership. However, in this case, like in so many cases before, God bypasses human customs to choose the person He wants. David is anointed as king before his family and in the eyes of the Lord, but it will be many years before he is publicly recognized as king. Meanwhile, not long after this private incident, Israel is engaged in a war with the Philistines. The Israeli and Philistine armies have gathered together on the field of battle. Sometimes in the ancient world a conflict would be decided by a duel between two champions, one from each army. In today's passage David's rise to prominence begins when he volunteers to combat the enemy's champion, the giant Goliath.

Pray for the Spirit's Insight

Read the Passage

Understanding the Passage

Why is Saul initially hesitant to allow David to fight Goliath?

Is David's confidence based on his own abilities or something else?

Questions for Further Consideration

What are some possible motivations for Saul giving David his armor in verse 38?

Related Bible Passages

Psalm 23

DAY 45

Scripture Reading: 1 Samuel 18: 1-9

Creation   Covenant   Christ   Church   Conclusion

Overview: Imagine two armies waiting for orders to begin combat against each other. Instead, the generals of the Philistine army elect to have the conflict decided by a duel. They put forward their champion, Goliath, who is described in the Bible as being "over nine feet tall (1 Samuel 17:4)." The giant, who is a seasoned warrior, challenges any man to come forward from Israel's ranks. No one comes forward. King Saul offers two great incentives to the man who can defeat the giant: great wealth and the hand of his daughter in marriage. Despite the prospects for instant status and riches, no one, not even King Saul's mighty warriors, come forward for this assignment. In ancient times the duel between the two fighters was seen as mirroring the battle between the two peoples' gods. The more powerful god's champion would win the battle. Thus, it was not only the reputation of Israel's fighting men, but the reputation of God himself that was at stake. David, while visiting his brothers at the battlefront, learns about this challenge from the Philistine giant. Saul is naturally hesitant to allow a shepherd boy to fight someone who out classes him in size and experience. However, David is confident that the Lord will grant Israel victory over her enemies including the giant Goliath. Saul, perhaps convinced by David's confidence in the Lord, or his experience in killing wild beasts, allows him to fight Goliath. David, unaccustomed to wearing armor, gives up the king's equipment to face the fully armed Philistine with his sling shot. David claims victory for Israel by killing the giant with a single stone and then cut's the giant's head off with his own sword. In today's passage we read about King Saul's reaction to David's rising reputation.

Pray for the Spirit's Insight

Read the Passage

Understanding the Passage

Do David and Jonathan, Saul's son, respect each other or hate each other?

How do the people react to David's victory and his new status in the army?

Questions for Further Consideration

Can you relate to Saul's jealously?

Related Bible Passages

Proverbs 27:4

DAY 46

Scripture Reading: 2 Samuel 5: 1-10

Creation   Covenant   Christ   Church   Conclusion

Overview: Saul is placed in a difficult situation as David's fame increases among the people of Israel. After defeating Goliath, David goes on to lead Israel in numerous victories against her enemies. Saul realizes that David is God's anointed servant to replace him as king. However, Saul isn't interested in losing his power. To complicate the situation for Saul, David is married to his daughter Michal, and best friends with his son Jonathan. Eventually, Saul begins to lose control over his hatred for David. Alerted by Jonathan of his father's murderous plan, David flees into the wilderness. For years David, with a small band of men, play a cat and mouse game with Saul and his forces. David, despite Saul's intentions, is unwilling to harm the person he describes as the Lord's anointed. On two occasions David even has the opportunity to kill Saul but refuses to do so (1 Sam. 24 and 26) and lets him go. In the meantime, the national situation has taken a turn for the worse during this period of infighting. The Philistines have returned in greater strength and King Saul and the army of Israel go to meet them in battle. During the course of the battle Saul is wounded, but out of pride, or perhaps fear, kills himself so as not to be taken captive by the enemy. Even Jonathan, David's best friend, is killed by the Philistines during the battle. After these events David goes on to execute justice over all parties involved in the conflict. He is ruthless with those he believes to be in the wrong with God and men, and beyond gracious to those deserving, including his former enemies. In today's passage we read about David's recognition as King over all of Israel.

Pray for the Spirit's Insight

Read the Passage

Understanding the Passage

What are the two reasons the elders give for making David king over all Israel?

What city does King David capture from the Jebusites?

Questions for Further Consideration

What is the reason the Bible gives for King David's growing power and influence?

Related Bible Passages

Psalm 89: 20-29

DAY 47

Scripture Reading: 2 Samuel 11: 1-11

Creation   Covenant   Christ   Church   Conclusion

Overview: The elders of Israel accept David's rule on the basis of his military experience as well as God's declaration through Samuel that David was to be the shepherd of Israel. It took years for David to realize his calling from God to be the king of the covenant people. He had to struggle, fight, and face numerous trials to be faithful to God's plan for his life. In our own lives of faith we must realize that personal gifting, passion, or a calling from God doesn't mean that we will not have to struggle in this world. In the midst of all of David's difficulties he remained faithful in seeking God's will. After become king of the whole country, David conquers the city of Jerusalem from the Jebusites. From this point forward Jerusalem becomes the geographical, political, and spiritual center of Israel. In future years the people of Israel grew to believe that a foreign people would never conquer David's city. They believed that God would protect the city from all attackers no matter the fate of the rest of Israel. An Old Testament perspective on life which is evident throughout the story of Israel, is that nothing happens, good or bad, that it is not guided by the hand of the Lord. Victories, despite the military prowess of soldiers and generals, were always ultimately attributed to God's power. The chief reason for David's success and power as king is stated in the previous passage, "because the Lord God Almighty was with him (2 Samuel 5:10)." As the years progress David goes on to defeat the Philistines and the Ammonites and to further solidify the borders of Israel. Israel enters a golden age of prosperity and near peace. In today's passage we read about David's encounter with a woman named Bathsheba.

Pray for the Spirit's Insight

Read the Passage

Understanding the Passage

Does the passage suggest that David wasn't where he was supposed to be?

When and where did David cross the moral line in this passage?

Questions for Further Consideration

How does David try to cover up his sin?

Related Bible Passages

Matthew 5:27-28

DAY 48

Scripture Reading: 2 Samuel 11: 12-27

Creation   Covenant   Christ   Church   Conclusion

Overview: David's brash disregard for God's commandments in his encounter with Bathsheba serves as a timeless reminder that even the faithful person can fall into grave sin. According to the previous passage, this incident took place during "the spring, at the time when kings go off to war," but the story goes on to add, "but David remained in Jerusalem." David's responsibilities lay with the army but instead he chose to stay home. The doorway to sin, that which separates us from God and each other, often creaks open when we do not carry out our God given responsibilities. A timeless question about the nature of sin is whether it begins with the actual act itself or in the person's mind long before the act takes place. One of the themes of Scripture is that sin begins inside the heart long before it ever manifests itself in behavior. It's difficult to know when David crossed the moral line. From a legalistic perspective, one could argue David crossed the line when he discovered that Bathsheba was married and summoned her to his private chambers anyway. From a Biblical perspective it could be argued that David crossed the moral line when he was gazing upon Bathsheba from the rooftop of his palace. To be faithful is not to live a life where one is never tempted, which would be impossible, but to flee temptations or seek to bring them to God when they come. Regardless, David abuses his power as king to get what he wants. A terrible situation is complicated by the fact that Bathsheba becomes pregnant. David tries to cover up his sin by arranging for Uriah to come home from the front line. In today's passage we read about David's final solution to the Bathsheba and Uriah problem.

Pray for the Spirit's Insight

Read the Passage

Understanding the Passage

Does King David's strategy of getting Uriah drunk work?

What is King David's final solution to the Bathsheba and Uriah problem?

Questions for Further Consideration

How do you think Bathsheba felt during this roller coast series of events?

Related Bible Passages

Leviticus 20:10

DAY 49

Scripture Reading: 1 Kings 1: 28-40

Creation   Covenant   Christ   Church   Conclusion

Overview: David summons Uriah, one of his own military officers, from the front line and encourages him to go home so that he will sleep with his wife. Much to David's frustration, Uriah refuses to take advantage of a special treatment that is not available to his comrades in the rest of the army, even when Uriah is drunk. Darkness had overcome David when he arranged for Uriah's death during battle. Uriah is killed by the Ammonites, opening a convenient door for David to make things "right" between himself and Bathsheba. He marries her and brings her into his house to live among his other wives and children. Not long after their marriage, the prophet Nathan confronts David about his sin (2 Samuel 12). Unlike King Saul, who never repented of his sins in breaking God's commandments, David does repent. He humbles himself through fasting and prayer. The illegitimate child dies, but later on Bathsheba and David have a son named Solomon, who will succeed his father as King of Israel. The years go on and David continues to secure the borders of Israel by winning wars against her national enemies. David desires to build a permanent temple for the Ark of the Covenant, but is informed by Nathan that it is God's will for his son Solomon to build the temple after his death. The transition from the rule of King David to his son Solomon does not take place without intrigue or struggle. David's eldest son, Absalom, attempts to undermine his father's rule and take the kingship of Israel for himself. Eventually, David is vindicated, Absalom is killed, and some stability is returned to the Kingdom. In today's passage we read about David, now elderly in years, talking to his wife Bathsheba about her their son Solomon.

Pray for the Spirit's Insight

Read the Passage

Understanding the Passage

What was the promise King David made to his wife Bathsheba?

Does anything strike you as odd about Solomon being the successor to David?

Questions for Further Consideration

What is the reaction of the people to the anointing of Solomon as king?

Related Bible Passages

1 Chronicles 29: 21-29

DAY 50

Scripture Reading: 1 Kings 11: 1-13

Creation   Covenant   Christ   Church   Conclusion

Overview: David advanced in age and coming close to death meets with his wife Bathsheba. Not long ago David's eldest son Absalom had attempted to claim the throne violently from his father. Forming the backdrop to the conversation between David and Bathsheba is the fact that a new challenger to the throne has arisen. This time David's fourth son, Adonijah, has attempted to claim the crown for himself. David, who is bedridden at this point, is unaware of Adonijah's activities until he is informed about them by the prophet Nathan. Bathsheba has come to visit David because she is afraid he will not keep his promise to her. David reassures Bathsheba that he will fulfill the promise he made to her that their son Solomon will succeed him as king. David then commands the priests and prophets to arrange for Solomon's public anointing as king, which is received with praise by the people. Considering the circumstances of David and Bathsheba's marriage, it is surprising that Solomon would be the son chosen to be Israel's king. God took a shameful and sinful situation and turned it around to bring new life and new possibilities for the whole nation of Israel in the reign of Solomon. Solomon's reign was characterized by great building programs, national peace, and prosperity. King Solomon, in an encounter with God, asked for wisdom and was granted it earning his reputation as the wisest person who ever lived (1 Kings 3). He built a great palace for himself as well as a permanent temple dedicated to the Lord in Jerusalem. Yet, in some ways Solomon was not like his father David. In today's passage we read about Solomon's failure to obey all of the commandments of the Lord.

Pray for the Spirit's Insight

Read the Passage

Understanding the Passage

What or who led Solomon astray from the ways of the Lord?

What commandment did Solomon specifically disobey?

Questions for Further Consideration

What are the consequences that Solomon will face for his actions?

Related Bible Passages

Deuteronomy 7: 1-4

DAY 51

Scripture Reading: 1 Kings 18: 16-29

Creation   Covenant   Christ   Church   Conclusion

Overview: In the reign of Solomon many saw the fulfillment of God's promise to Abraham that "I will make you into a great nation" (Genesis 12:2). The city of Jerusalem was blessed by housing the dwelling place of God's special presence in the new temple built by Solomon. Yet, Solomon despite his wisdom breaks the first commandment of the Law, "You shall have no other gods before me" (Exodus 20:2). In ancient times it was customary for men to have multiple wives. This was more for economic reasons than for the unbridled pleasure of a man. However, it was not unusual for powerful men, especially kings, to have concubines for their own pleasure. King David himself had several wives, probably numbering fewer than a dozen. Solomon's dazzling number of wives and concubines, reaching 1000 in number, seems vastly extravagant. Solomon was so influenced by these women that he began to establish places of worship for their gods. The Lord informs Solomon that because of his disobedience the majority of the kingdom will be taken away from his descendents. After Solomon's death, civil war breaks out and the nation is divided into two parts, the northern and southern kingdoms. Prophets, in the tradition of Samuel and Nathan, are sent to deliver God's message to the disobedient kings of the Kingdom of Israel and the Kingdom of Judah (where David's descendants continued to reign). Today's passage occurs during the reign of King Ahab and Queen Jezebel who had arranged for the death of most of God's prophets. The reading recalls a contest between the pagan priests of Baal (the god favored by Jezebel) and the last remaining prophet of the Lord, Elijah.

Pray for the Spirit's Insight

Read the Passage

Understanding the Passage

What is the purpose of the contest that Elijah establishes?

What do you think of Elijah's comments in verse 27?

Questions for Further Consideration

Do the prophets of Baal and Asherah receive a response from their gods?

Related Bible Passages

Romans 11: 1-4

DAY 52

Scripture Reading: 1 Kings 18: 30-39

Creation   Covenant   Christ   Church   Conclusion

Overview: The prophet Elijah was a remarkable figure in the Old Testament, not only boldly speaking the word of the Lord, but also performing miracles by the power of God. For the most part, prophets were on the fringes of Israeli society. The power centers of Israel were the royal court and the temple priesthood. However, even the priests, during the time of the kings, were often corrupt and not committed to following God's ways. A prophet would receive a message from God for the entire nation or in some cases for a particular person. Delivering these messages was dangerous because usually the message from God condemned the unfaithful behavior of the people and their rulers. For example, during the time of Elijah the leaders of Israel had hunted down all of the prophets of God and had them killed. The principal problem that God's people, in both kingdoms, continued to face, was the threat of worshipping other gods. Again and again, despite the prophets' warnings, the people, usually led by their king, abandoned the God of Abraham and worshiped pagan gods. In a scenario echoing the battle between the gods of Egypt and the God of Israel (Exodus 7-11), Elijah challenges the pagan fertility god Baal to a contest. As in Egypt, the purpose of the battle is to prove that there is only one Lord, the God of Israel. The priests of Baal, despite their gruesome rituals, get no response from their god. Elijah takes this opportunity to taunt his enemies with questions about the power and existence of Baal. In today's passage we read about the response Elijah receives from God.

Pray for the Spirit's Insight

Read the Passage

Understanding the Passage

Why do you think Elijah orders water to be poured on the offering?

Why does Elijah want God to answer his prayer?

Questions for Further Consideration

What is the reaction of the people to the Lord's fire consuming the offering?

Related Bible Passages

Psalm 115: 1-8

DAY 53

Scripture Reading: 2 Kings 17: 1-15

Creation   Covenant   Christ   Church   Conclusion

Overview: After the pagan priests failed to receive a response from Baal the prophet of the Lord orders jars of water to be poured out on his sacrificial offering. Elijah orders the pouring out of the water on the sacrifice for the same reason God lowered the number of Gideon's army centuries earlier. The purpose was to make sure that it was God, and not Elijah, who would get the ultimate glory for the victory over Baal. Also, because the sacrifice was drenched with water there would be no room for anyone to argue that it caught fire by accident. Elijah's interest in this divine contest was less about showing off his status as a miracle working prophet and more about reaching the wayward people of Israel. The victor of the contest was unmistakable and the people of Israel declared, "The Lord — he is God! The Lord — he is God" (1 Kings 18:39). While Elijah was victorious in this encounter, the people did not return to the Lord. As the decades and centuries passed kings came and went in both the northern (Israel) and southern (Judah, David's line) kingdoms. All of the kings that reigned in Israel led their people away from following God's ways. Conversely, there was a handful of faithful kings in Judah that worked to bring reform and return to the God of Abraham. During this time period, often referred to as the divided kingdom, the ministry of the prophets reached its height. Prophets like Isaiah, Jeremiah, and others pleaded with their kings and fellow Israelites to return to the ways of God. In most cases the preaching of the prophets was ignored but not without consequence. In today's passage we read about the consequences that the people of the Northern Kingdom faced for abandoning their covenant with God.

Pray for the Spirit's Insight

Read the Passage

Understanding the Passage

According to the passage what kind of ruler was King Hoshea?

What prompted Assyria to invade the Northern Kingdom?

Questions for Further Consideration

What was the main reason, according to the text, that Israel was conquered?

Related Bible Passages

Deuteronomy 28: 58-68

DAY 54

Scripture Reading: Isaiah 42: 1-9

Creation   Covenant   Christ   Church   Conclusion

Overview: The previous passage describes Hoshea as someone who "did evil in the eyes of the Lord (2 Kings 17:2). While the invasion of Assyria is prompted by the discovery of Hoshea's foreign policy scandal, the responsibility for the fall of Israel can best be attributed to all of the people of Israel together. Specifically, the people in the northern kingdom (Israel) had abandoned the covenant that God had made with their ancestors. They had worshipped false gods, which clearly violated the teaching of the covenant. While God had acquiesced to the people of Israel in granting them a king, they were still to trust in God for their ultimate protection. The actions of kings like Hoshea, in making treaties with foreign nations, did not please God. The irony of Hoshea making a treaty with Egypt is a tragic one because that decision leads Israel to become enslaved to the Assyrian Empire. A standard practice in military conquest in the ancient world was to resettle large segments of a native population to another part of the empire. This ensured that the newly conquered territory would be destabilized and unlikely to rebel. To the average Israeli this must have been a sign that God had abandoned them. This was the land that their God had promised to them forever (Genesis 17:8). Despite the dark days of the Assyrian captivity, a message of hope had begun to surface in the preaching of the prophets. This was a messianic hope, anticipating that one-day, a faithful king, of David's line, would return and establish God's people as a righteous kingdom. In today's passage we read from the preaching of the prophet Isaiah, who ministered to the kingdom of Judah (southern kingdom) about this messianic hope.

Pray for the Spirit's Insight

Read the Passage

Understanding the Passage

What will God do through His "chosen one" as described in the passage?

What will some of the character traits of this person be?

Questions for Further Consideration

Is there any indication that this passage is making a prediction about the future?

Related Bible Passages

Matthew 12: 18-21

DAY 55

Scripture Reading: Isaiah 58: 1-14

Creation   Covenant   Christ   Church   Conclusion

Overview: In his poetic style, typical of Isaiah, the prophet describes an individual that the Old Testament sometimes refers to as "the servant of the Lord." In many ways the description of this individual is an antithesis of the characteristics typical of the vast majority of Israel's and Judah's kings. Unlike them he will establish justice in the land (Isaiah 42:4) and will be faithful to the ways of the Lord (42:3). Through this special person the promise to Abraham will be fulfilled that Israel will become "a light for the Gentiles (42:6)," gentiles being non-Jews. Scattered across the Old Testament, especially in the prophets and the Psalms, are passages that refer to this coming servant of the Lord. It took centuries for God's people to build upon these Biblical foundations to understand that one day a Messiah-King would come and restore Israel to her rightful place as God's chosen nation. This Messiah would have to come from David's line, for David was Israel's greatest king, and the Spirit of God was on him (42:1). Isaiah, like the rest of the Old Testament, gives no specific information as to when the Messiah will arrive but only proclaims that He will come (42:9). Over the centuries, as God's chosen people faced many hardships, the longing for the coming of the Messiah increased. The preaching of Isaiah and the other prophets was not limited to judgment on pagan worship or to the hope that one-day, a Messiah would come. Following the God of Abraham, Isaac, and Jacob involved more than carrying out the correct religious services and rituals as described in the Torah (see Leviticus). In today's passage we read about the lifestyle of justice that the people of God are to manifest in their relationships with others.

Pray for the Spirit's Insight

Read the Passage

Understanding the Passage

Why is God not pleased by the fasting of His people?

What is the kind of fasting that God is pleased with?

Questions for Further Consideration

How do you think this passage might speak to our contemporary society?

Related Bible Passages

Matthew 25: 34-40

DAY 56

Scripture Reading: Jeremiah 38: 14-28

Creation   Covenant   Christ   Church   Conclusion

Overview: During the period of the divided kingdoms the people of God sometimes experienced seasons of relative prosperity and peace. During these times they often made great sacrifices and celebrations to the Lord God. However, the prophets often condemned such celebrations as mere religious observances instead of the wholehearted devotion to holy living that the Lord required. Under God's direction Isaiah criticizes the fasting and religious ceremonies of the people. Isaiah was not against fasting, the temple sacrifices, or other celebrations dedicated to the Lord. However, what infuriated Isaiah and displeased God was that despite all this religious activity, the poor, enslaved, and hungry were being ignored. The kind of fasting that pleases God, according to Isaiah is "to loose the chains of injustice and untie the cords of the yoke, to set the oppressed free (Isaiah 58:6)." Religious services, sacrifices, and rituals are important, but unless they lead to right thinking and action they mean nothing according to the prophet (58:4). The words of the prophets continue to be used by God to inspire justice in our world today. The previous passage alone could address dozens of problems in our own societies, families, and churches. If we are to be followers of the God that is revealed in the pages of Scripture, we cannot ignore matters of justice. Despite the preaching of the prophets and the fall of Israel, the southern kingdom of Judah did not reform her ways. The prophet Jeremiah ministered in Judah for many long years. He was not a popular man because his message was one of doom for the people of Judah. In today's reading we learn about an encounter Jeremiah had with the last king of Judah, Zedekiah.

Pray for the Spirit's Insight

Read the Passage

Understanding the Passage

What kind of relationship does Jeremiah appear to have with King Zedekiah?

What message does Jeremiah give to Zedekiah regarding the Babylonians?

Questions for Further Consideration

Do you think Zedekiah will listen to the message from Jeremiah?

Related Bible Passages
Proverbs 29:25

DAY 57

Scripture Reading: Jeremiah 39: 1-10

Creation   Covenant   Christ   Church   Conclusion

Overview: The relationship between Jeremiah and the various administrations of the Kingdom of Judah was tenuous at best. Except for King Josiah, who had been faithful to the Lord (2 Chronicles 34:1-2), the rest of the kings of Judah opposed Jeremiah. While the court prophets, on salary from the royal palace, would often prophecy in favor of the kings' decisions, Jeremiah would always be faithful in delivering God's message. Usually Jeremiah delivered bad news and information that opposed the king. In the previous passage Jeremiah is under arrest in the royal palace because of his preaching ministry. However, even King Zedekiah is aware that Jeremiah is a legitimate prophet of the Lord and seeks out his counsel. Jerusalem, David's city, the city that could never be captured, was in a grievous situation. While the Assyrian Empire had declined over the years, it was now the Babylonian Empire that was threatening the freedom of Judah and her capital city. Jeremiah, after being reassured that he would not be killed for communicating God's message, informs Zedekiah that Babylon will be the victor. The prophet goes on to offer the king two options. He can surrender to Babylon and save Jerusalem and himself, or he can resist Babylon and lose Jerusalem and his own life. Zedekiah is doubly frightened by Jeremiah's message and is unsure of what action to take. On the one hand the king is afraid of the group of Jews that has defected to the Babylonians. He is worried that if he surrenders he will end up being placed in their custody. Conversely, the potential of being the king who would lose David's city, and his own life in the process, must have also burdened Zedekiah's thoughts. In today's passage we read about the fate of Jerusalem in the hands of the Babylonian army.

Pray for the Spirit's Insight

Read the Passage

Understanding the Passage

What happens to the city of Jerusalem?

What happens to King Zedekiah?

Questions for Further Consideration

What happens to many of the Jews living in Judah?

Related Bible Passages
2 Kings 25:8-12

DAY 58

Scripture Reading: Ezra 1: 1-11

Creation   Covenant   Christ   Church   Conclusion

Overview: King Zedekiah does not heed the words of Jeremiah the prophet. The army of the Babylonian Empire easily takes the city of Jerusalem. The walls of Jerusalem are destroyed, and while not mentioned in the previous passage, the Temple of the Lord is also leveled to the ground. Many of God's people are taken into exile to Babylon to live in a foreign culture that does not live by the teachings of the Law. For many, the fall of Jerusalem and the Kingdom of Judah must have signaled the end of God's covenant with their ancestor Abraham. Israel, the Northern Kingdom, had already been destroyed, and now David's city and the great temple were no more. The land that God had promised to Abraham and his descendants was no longer in the hands of God's people. The Babylonian exile in many ways echoed the foundational exile between God and His people that took place in the Garden of Eden (Genesis 3). The promise land was to be a second Eden of sorts where God and the covenant people could live in harmony, love, and full relationship. In the Garden, the boundary was to not eat of the tree of the knowledge of good and evil. In the Holy Land, the boundary was to not worship other gods and follow their ways. Despite God's faithfulness, Adam and Eve and their descendents could not avoid crossing the boundaries established by the Lord. Sin, that which separates us from God, from each other, and from ourselves, continued to plague the human condition with no solution in sight. God was so unapproachable that the majority of the people could not follow Him faithfully. In today's passage, seventy years after the Babylonian victory, we read about the beginnings of the restoration of Jerusalem.

Pray for the Spirit's Insight

Read the Passage

Understanding the Passage

What does Cyrus, King of Persia, command to be rebuilt in Jerusalem?

What people are allowed to return to Jerusalem?

Questions for Further Consideration

If you were a Jew in the exile, how do you think you would react to this news?

Related Bible Passages

Jeremiah 25: 11-12

DAY 59

Scripture Reading: Ezra 3: 7-13

Creation   Covenant   Christ   Church   Conclusion

Overview: After seventy years of exile, in a foreign land, God's people are given the opportunity to return to the Promised Land. The fall of Israel, in both the southern and northern kingdoms, came about slowly over several generations. The prophets, and the few faithful kings of Judah, encouraged each generation to return to the ways of the Lord. Despite this, people violated God's commandments and eventually found themselves living in a foreign land. Many believed God had abandoned the covenant He made with them, but others believed that the Lord would be faithful and restore Israel. When Cyrus, ruler of the Persian Empire (which had eclipsed the Babylonian Empire in importance), gave the order to rebuild the Temple in Jerusalem, many Jews saw this as a sign of God's faithfulness to the covenant. Cyrus's official edict declared that, "anyone one of...you...may...go up to Jerusalem (Ezra 1:3)." Thousands of exiled Jews began the journey south to resettle the Promise Land. Ezra, himself an exile, was a priest and teacher of the Law. He was one of the leaders of the resettlement movement in the return from the Babylonian exile. Many of God's commandments concerned the observing of feasts and the offering of sacrifices (see Leviticus). These feasts and sacrifices could only be performed in the Temple in Jerusalem. Further, they could only be performed by Jewish priests, men like Ezra, who were descendents of Moses' brother, Aaron (Exodus 28:1-5). The Babylonian exile not only tore people away from their homes, but also impaired them from being able to worship God fully. In today's passage we read about the rebuilding of the Temple.

Pray for the Spirit's Insight

Read the Passage

Understanding the Passage

Who supervised the rebuilding of the Temple?

How did the people react to the construction of the new temple foundation?

Questions for Further Consideration

How would you explain the mixed reactions of joy and weeping in verse 12?

Related Bible Passages

Psalm 126

DAY 60

Scripture Reading: Ezra 6: 13-22

Creation   Covenant   Christ   Church   Conclusion

Overview: The construction of the second Temple was supervised by the Levite (assistants to the priests) and priestly families. The building materials necessary for the Temple construction were brought in from across the Empire. The Temple, especially the first temple built by King Solomon (1 Kings 6), was an impressive structure with many elaborate details constructed by many craftsmen. The Temple was believed to be a sacred structure that housed the presence of the Lord in a special way. Once completed, it would be the place where the sacrifices and sacred festivals were observed. In addition, certain parts of the Temple were reserved for particular kinds of people. The outer courtyard of the Temple was sometimes referred to as the court of the Gentiles. Here anyone could come to pray and honor the God of Israel. The next layer of the Temple was the courtyard of the women. This was as far as Jewish women could go inside the Temple, and it was here that they would offer their prayers. The next area of the temple was where Jewish men could come for prayer and to give the priests their sacrifices. Inside the temple itself was an area where only priests could go, and then finally there was a small room called the Holy of Holies. Here, only the Jewish high priest could go once per year on the Feast of the Atonement or what is commonly known today as Yom Kippur (Leviticus 16). The laying of the new foundation for the reconstruction of the Temple was met with both joyful shouts and tears. Present on this occasion were elders who had seen the first temple when they were children. In today's passage we read about the completion and dedication of the second temple.

Pray for the Spirit's Insight

Read the Passage

Understanding the Passage

Did the ministry of prophets continue after the exile?

What does it mean in verse 20 when it says the priests made themselves clean?

Questions for Further Consideration

After the dedication of the Temple, what religious feast did the people observe?

Related Bible Passages

Exodus 12:1-30

DAY 61

Scripture Reading: Luke 1: 26-38

Creation   Covenant   Christ   Church   Conclusion

Overview: Eventually the temple was rebuilt despite, the efforts of some to oppose its reconstruction (Ezra 4). It was a glorious day celebrated by all of the people and confirmation for many that God had not abandoned His people. The ministry of the prophets continued throughout the exile and into the early years of resettlement. Associated with Biblical Judaism, and specifically the temple, was the idea of ceremonially purity. The Law contains several guidelines that Jewish men and women must observe in order to be clean (see Leviticus). This kind of cleanliness is not of a physical nature but of a spiritual nature. If an individual was not clean, they were prevented from participating in certain community activities, such as worship. The sacrifices prescribed in the Law of Moses were intended to be offered to God in order that a person might be forgiven of their sin, made clean, and brought back into right relationship with God. The central thrust of this spiritual cleanliness in the Old Testament was to emphasize that the people of Israel were a distinct people. After Ezra, in the coming centuries Israel would mostly be a captive nation. One super power after another would wrestle for the strategic plot of land that Israel occupied in the Middle East. During the New Testament period Israel was occupied by the powerful Roman Empire, and many people in Israel were hoping that God's chosen one, the Messiah, would return and overthrow the Roman government. People longed to hear a fresh Word from God as it had been centuries since the last of the prophets had died. In today's passage we read about the unlikely fulfillment of God's promises to Israel through a teenage girl.

Pray for the Spirit's Insight

Read the Passage

Understanding the Passage

What is the news that the angel Gabriel delivers to Mary?

Can you detect any echoes of the Old Testament in this passage?

Questions for Further Consideration

How would you react if you were in Mary's place?

Related Bible Passages

Matthew 1

DAY 62

Scripture Reading: Luke 2: 1-20

Creation   Covenant   Christ   Church   Conclusion

Overview: In the previous passage we met Mary, a Jewish girl who was living in 1st century Israel. The powerful Roman Empire occupied her country and she was pledged to be married to a carpenter named Joseph. Suddenly, her life is turned upside down when God's messenger, Gabriel, appears to her delivering a fantastic message. Mary is not the first woman to receive a divine message regarding her child. Echoes of the Old Testament stories of Abraham and Sarah (Genesis 18), Isaac and Rebekah (Genesis 25), Jacob and Rachel (Genesis 29), as well as Hannah, and the birth her son Samuel (1 Samuel 1), can be found in the previous passage. In fact, Mary's older relative, Elizabeth, has become pregnant in her old age through God's intervention (Luke 1:24). However, unlike all of the previous women, Mary is a virgin. The child that she will give birth to will be fathered by the power of Holy Spirit (Luke 1:35). In a society where pregnancy outside of marriage was not tolerated and could result in death if discovered, Mary could have received this news negatively. Instead, setting an example for Christians for all time, she responded to the angel's message by saying yes. In our own Christian lives we sometimes wonder how God will deliver on the promise He has given us. We can take our cues from Mary, the teenage girl who, despite not knowing what lay ahead for her, or her child, simply said "I am the Lord's servant" and "May it be to me as you have said." Initially, her betrothed, Joseph, struggles with this news and decides to quietly divorce her, but he changes his mind after an angel speaks to him in a dream (Matthew 1:19-21). In today's passage we read about the circumstances surrounding the birth of Jesus.

Pray for the Spirit's Insight

Read the Passage

Understanding the Passage

Whose family were Joseph and Mary descended from? Why is this important?

Where is Jesus born? In a palace or a castle? Why is this important?

Questions for Further Consideration

Who are the first witnesses to the birth of Jesus? Why is this important?

Related Bible Passages

John 1:1-18

DAY 63

Scripture Reading: Luke 3: 1-9, 15-19

Creation   Covenant   Christ   Church   Conclusion

Overview: When the Emperor spoke, ordinary people did as they were told. Joseph and Mary were both of the house of David and therefore had to go to Bethlehem, the birthplace and hometown of David, to be registered. If the child to be born was truly the Messiah, he would have to be descended from King David and born in Bethlehem to fulfill Old Testament prophecy (Micah 5:2). The small country town of Bethlehem was overwhelmed with visitors because of the edict from Augustus Caesar. Therefore, Mary and Joseph were unable to secure any kind of regular accommodations, such as a room in the local inn (Luke 1:7). This forced them to find shelter in a stable. In the stable, Mary gave birth to Jesus and laid him in a manager, which was normally used as a feeding trough for animals. God's angelic messengers first reveal the news of Jesus' birth, not to the powerful personalities of the first century, but to shepherds tending their flocks in the fields. God was doing something unthinkable in the minds of most people, including the minds of the religious leaders of Israel. God was bringing the Messiah, His only beloved Son, into the world not with great fanfare but in humility. The fact, that the Son of God entered the world as a poor baby boy in a smelly stable sent the message that God was going to be in relationship to all of His people, regardless of their social status. In the past people tried obeying the Law to reach upwards to God. In Jesus God reached down to humanity and dwelt among His people, which is the literal meaning of Jesus' name, Immanuel, "God with us." In today's passage, roughly 30 years later, we read about John the Baptist and his ministry of preparing Israel for the coming of the Messiah.

Pray for the Spirit's Insight

Read the Passage

Understanding the Passage

What was the central message of John's preaching?

How did John reply when asked if he was the Messiah?

Questions for Further Consideration

Did everyone respect and respond positively to John's preaching?

Related Bible Passages

John 1:19-34

DAY 64

Scripture Reading: Luke 3: 21-38

Creation   Covenant   Christ   Church   Conclusion

Overview: Many people saw the qualities of an Old Testament prophet in John the Baptist. Prophets, like John, were often on the fringes of society and usually delivered messages calling for repentance. John called upon Israel to reform her ways and return to God. In the Old Testament, prophets like Isaiah and Jeremiah warned the people of God's coming judgment in the form of conquering armies from Assyria or Babylon. John's message was different in that he was warning Israel to prepare for the coming of an individual. In preparation for the coming Messiah, John challenged the crowds to repent of their sins and live rightly according to God's ways. John saw his calling from God as one who was to prepare others to receive and meet the coming Savior. Even later on when Jesus' ministry began to grow, even as his own ministry declined, John remained assured of his purpose. He told his own followers, regarding Jesus, "He must increase, I must decrease (John 3:30)." As contemporary followers of God we would do well to take John the Baptist as our example in working with others in their spiritual lives. At first we might be very important in a person's life, but the end goal is that the person has a saving relationship with Christ and not with us. Often our role in that person's life must decrease as their own spiritual life increases. Not everyone was pleased with the preaching of John the Baptist. Herod, who was one of the regional rulers of Israel, was annoyed with John's preaching because it condemned him for breaking the Law by divorcing his wife so he could marry his own niece (who was already married to his brother!). In today's passage we read about Jesus' baptism by John.

Pray for the Spirit's Insight

Read the Passage

Understanding the Passage

Why would Jesus need to be baptized by John?

What happens after Jesus is baptized?

Questions for Further Consideration

What is important about the genealogy table included in the passage?

Related Bible Passages

Matthew 3:13-17

DAY 65

Scripture Reading: Luke 4: 1-13

Creation   Covenant   Christ   Church   Conclusion

Overview: In Judaism there were ceremonies similar to baptism, which would often be repeated many times, for the purposes of achieving ceremonial purity. John's baptism was a sign of a person's repentance and desire to live life differently. After the ministry of Jesus, baptism in the Christian tradition came to be associated with the burial, death, and resurrection of Jesus. Jesus' baptism by John the Baptist could be understood in several ways. However, the chief explanation that may be helpful to understand it is that through John the Baptist the story of God in the Old Testament is connected to the story of God in the New Testament. John is the last of the Old Testament prophets because Jesus, a person greater than a prophet, has arrived. While God is doing something new in the person of Jesus, He is not doing something disconnected from what He has done in the past. As Jesus emerges out of the waters of the Jordan River, a voice speaks from the heavens saying, "You are my Son, whom I love; with you I am well pleased (Luke 3:22)." Jesus baptism in the Jordan River serves as a marker of the beginning of his public ministry as the Messiah. In the previous passage there is a genealogy table following the account of Jesus baptism. While Luke acknowledges that Jesus was not Joseph's biological son (Luke 3:23), the book does provide a listing of Jesus' ancestry from his stepfather's side. This table shows that Jesus is directly connected to all of the great Old Testament heroes of the faith from King David, to Abraham, Isaac, and Jacob, and even Adam. Jesus, while flesh and blood, is also divine. In today's passage we read about Jesus' temptation in the desert.

Pray for the Spirit's Insight

Read the Passage

Understanding the Passage

What happens to Jesus after he is baptized?

Who challenges Jesus to be unfaithful to God in the desert?

Questions for Further Consideration

Do you hear any echoes of the Old Testament in Jesus' wilderness temptation?

Related Bible Passages

Matthew 4:1-11

DAY 66

Scripture Reading: Luke 5: 1-11

Creation   Covenant   Christ   Church   Conclusion

Overview: The Scriptures declare that after his baptism Jesus was "full of the Holy Spirit" but was immediately driven by the Spirit into the desert. For forty days and nights Jesus goes without food and is tempted by Satan. In the Bible Satan is seen as a fallen angel, a being far less powerful than God, who rebelled against the Lord and whose chief power lies in his ability to deceive. In the Scriptures Satan is often understood to be the chief spiritual power of this fallen world. That is to say, that in a world which is disconnected from God (Genesis 3) an unhealthy spiritual power will have the ability to rule. Satan's main strategy is to get Jesus to act contrary to God's will. If you read carefully and consider earlier parts of the Bible, several echoes of the Old Testament are evident in this passage. In the New Testament Jesus is seen as the faithful son of Israel that God's people in the Old Testament never were. During their forty years in the desert the Israelites complained about the food God provided, worshiped other gods, and constantly tested their relationship with the Lord. They failed to keep the covenant that God had established with Abraham, Isaac, and Jacob. Through Jesus, humanity is finally able to keep the covenant and enjoy a full relationship with God. After his temptation Jesus returns to his hometown of Nazareth, where he grew up, to begin his public ministry. From there Jesus goes to travel throughout Galilee, a rural area in Israel, performing miraculous healings (Luke 4:40) and casting out demons (Luke 4:35). In today's passage we read about the calling of Jesus' first disciples.

Pray for the Spirit's Insight

Read the Passage

Understanding the Passage

From what location is Jesus teaching in this passage?

What is Simon's response to Jesus' suggestion in verse 4?

Questions for Further Consideration

How would you react, if you were Simon, to Jesus' statement in verse 10?

Related Bible Passages

John 1:35-42

DAY 67

Scripture Reading: Luke 5: 17-26

Creation   Covenant   Christ   Church   Conclusion

Overview: In the previous passage Jesus walks upon the shores of the Sea of Galilee, which is actually a large fresh water lake, and sits down inside a boat. The boat is owned by Simon (later called Peter) and his business associates. After he had finished teaching the people, he told Simon to "put out into deep water, and let down the nets for a catch." Simon and his friends had been fishing all night. At this point, probably sometime in the morning, they were disheartened after catching nothing. However, Simon Peter agreed to do as Jesus instructed. It's difficult to speculate as to why Simon did this. Perhaps he didn't want to disrespect the traveling Rabbi (Jesus) in front of the crowd. Perhaps, God was already working in Peter's heart to prepare him to say yes to Jesus subsequent invitation to discipleship. The result of their effort is that a miraculous load of fish is caught. In the midst of the wonder and excitement that must have taken place during this event, Peter has a reflective moment. He feels unworthy of Jesus' presence and perhaps even frightened by what was happened. It is clear to Peter that something out of the ordinary, something supernatural and spiritual, has just occurred. Then Jesus tells him and his friends, "Don't be afraid, from now on you will catch men (Luke 5:10)." Today Jesus is making the same invitation to every person in the world, regardless of their age, gender, or station in life; Jesus is asking you to "catch people," and to follow Him. Peter and the other first disciples had no idea how their lives would be changed by following Jesus. Yet, they made the key choice that all of us must make in life, who will we follow? In today's passage we read about Jesus and his encounter with a paralyzed man.

Pray for the Spirit's Insight

Read the Passage

Understanding the Passage

In this passage some other religious leaders appear. Who are they?

How does Jesus help the paralytic?

Questions for Further Consideration

Is everyone pleased with what Jesus has done for the paralytic?

Related Bible Passages

Matthew 9:1-8

DAY 68

Scripture Reading: Luke 6: 17-26

Creation   Covenant   Christ   Church   Conclusion

Overview: Jesus' reputation as a faith healer quickly spread across Galilee into the rest of Israel. Jesus spent the majority of his ministry in rural Galilee. The people he taught were regular men and women and his chosen disciples were unlike the highly educated students of the Pharisees. In the previous passage we read about the Pharisees having a disagreement with Jesus. The Pharisees were religious leaders, what we might think of as the precursors to our idea of rabbis, who taught the common people the Law of Moses. They were experts in the Old Testament and were committed to living holy lives before God. The Pharisees were not temple priests. The Sadducees were the priests whose chief concerns were related to the worship life of the temple. Not all of the Pharisees opposed Jesus, but many disagreed with him. In the previous passage some men brought their paralyzed friend to Jesus. Jesus then claimed to have forgiven the man's sins (Luke 5: 20). The Pharisees found this claim offensive. Being good students of the Bible they knew that no one but God alone can forgive someone of his or her sins. Jesus, aware of their concerns then commanded the man to stand up and take up his mat and go home (Luke 5:24). By healing the man Jesus proves his point that the "Son of Man" has the power to forgive sins. This action demonstrated Jesus divinity as the Son of God. Over the course of his ministry Jesus got in trouble with the religious leaders over his claims to be in a special, divine, relationship with the Father. In today's passage we encounter Jesus acting as a teacher and prophet. He is interacting with concepts found in the Old Testament but is stating them in new and fresher ways.

Pray for the Spirit's Insight

Read the Passage

Understanding the Passage

In this passage what happens before Jesus starts teaching?

How do you think Jesus' listeners would have responded to his message?

Questions for Further Consideration

Which teaching in this passage do you find most comforting or challenging?

Related Bible Passages

Matthew 5-7

DAY 69

Scripture Reading: Luke 7: 1-11

Creation   Covenant   Christ   Church   Conclusion

Overview: After healing the paralytic, Jesus continues his ministry of preaching from town to town. He continues to get into disagreements with the Pharisees about such topics as observing the Sabbath (Luke 6) and fasting (Luke 5:33). Jesus was a charismatic figure, and many men and women committed themselves to being his disciples. Just prior to our last passage, Jesus selected twelve of these disciples to serve as apostles (Luke 6:12-16). The apostles served as Jesus' inner circle of trust and as leaders for the rest of the discipleship movement. Out in the open air Jesus finds a large place where he addresses his disciples. Much of what Jesus said would have been familiar to his Jewish listeners. The format in which he delivered his message echoed the blessings and curses found in the Torah (Deuteronomy 30: 11-20) as well as the preaching of the prophets. However, the reaction to Jesus' message likely varied from listener to listener. Some of his teachings went against traditional beliefs of how God interacts with His people. Wealth, comfort, and a good reputation were understood by many to be a sign of God's blessing. Conversely, poverty, mourning, and persecution were thought be signs of God's disappointment with someone. Jesus flipped many of these ideas over by promising the poor the inheritance of God's kingdom (Luke 6:20). Jesus was not abandoning the teachings of the Old Testament, but saw Himself as fulfilling them (Matthew 5:17). Jesus' teaching strongly echoed the passionate preaching of the prophets with their concerns for practical justice. In today's passage we read about a non-Jew, a Roman military officer, and his request of Jesus.

Pray for the Spirit's Insight

Read the Passage

Understanding the Passage

Can you tell if this Roman officer is a man respected by the Jewish community?

Does Jesus agree to the Centurion's request?

Questions for Further Consideration

Why might some of Jesus' listeners been offended by his comment in verse 9?

Related Bible Passages

Matthew 8:5-13

DAY 70

Scripture Reading: Luke 8: 1-15

Creation   Covenant   Christ   Church   Conclusion

Overview: In Capernaum the Jewish elders ask Jesus to help out a Roman army officer. This Centurion must have been a particularly pious man. Remember, the Roman Empire was in control of Israel, and this solider was part of the occupying force that kept Israel pacified. There were non-Jews who became influenced by Judaism in the time of Jesus. They admired the Jewish way of life and found wisdom in worshiping only one God, as opposed to the many gods of the pagan religions. They were titled "God fearers", and strove to live a life according to God's ways without actually becoming Jews themselves. Some groups in Israel would have nothing to do with gentiles and Romans in particular. These groups, such as the guerilla fighters known as the Zealots, regarded Jews who interacted with gentiles, even "God fearers," as compromisers of the faith. Jesus agrees to help this man but is astonished at his response. The Roman officer has such great faith in Jesus' authority that he believes Jesus can heal his servant without actually visiting him. Jesus' response, "I have not found such great faith even in Israel! (Luke 7:9), "must have offended many people. The people of Israel were God's chosen people. Israel received the Law from God. Israel was set free from slavery by God's power in Egypt. Yet, the original purpose for Israel was to establish a priestly nation to bring God's message to all people (Genesis 12:3). In this encounter, and others, Jesus begins to foreshadow that in God's coming kingdom Jew and Gentile alike will be welcome. In today's passage we learn more about Jesus' teaching style through his use of parables.

Pray for the Spirit's Insight

Read the Passage

Understanding the Passage

What does this passage tell you about the role of women in Jesus' ministry?

According to the passage, why won't everyone understand Jesus' message?

Questions for Further Consideration

Where would you place yourself in this parable, which group of seeds?

Related Bible Passages

Mark 4:1-10

DAY 71

Scripture Reading: Luke 9: 1-9

Creation   Covenant   Christ   Church   Conclusion

Overview: In the previous passage we learned that many women were included among Jesus' disciples. In fact, it was these women, and others, who financially supported Jesus' ministry (Luke 8:3). Beyond this, Jesus taught both men and women publicly (Luke 6:20) and privately (Luke 10:39). In the Kingdom of God, which was Jesus' central message, men and women would speak and be guided by God's spirit. In the previous passage Jesus teaches one of his most famous parables to a crowd of people. Afterwards in private the disciples ask Jesus why it is that he speaks in parables. Parables are stories told to communicate a religious truth. They employ metaphors and similes to draw a picture of what God or His kingdom is like. Jesus' reply is somewhat cryptic seeming to indicate that not everyone will understand His message (Luke 8:10). Matters of faith and spirituality involve more than an intellectual understanding. Many of Jesus' opponents knew the information that was in the Scriptures far better than the apostles. Yet, it was they, not his opponents, who grew to understand who and what Jesus was all about. In our own lives of faith we must not neglect our intellect but realize that to truly understand God's ways will require a personal relationship with Him. In different seasons of our lives we might be able to find ourselves in different kinds of spiritual soil. Yet, our goal should be to become like the seed that falls into the good soil (Luke 10:15). To do this we must make sure we are regularly being watered by God's Word, spiritual friendships, and prayerful conversation with Christ. In today's passage we read about how Jesus empowered his apostles to carry out God's mission in the world.

Pray for the Spirit's Insight

Read the Passage

Understanding the Passage

How did Jesus empower the apostles to carry out God's mission?

What does Jesus tell the apostles to do when their message is rejected?

Questions for Further Consideration

What kind of rumors were starting to spread in Israel about Jesus?

Related Bible Passages

Matthew 10:1-42

DAY 72

Scripture Reading: Luke 9: 18-27

Creation   Covenant   Christ   Church   Conclusion

Overview: After explaining the parable of the sower, Jesus teaches on the radical nature of human relationships in God's Kingdom (Luke 8:21) and then awes the disciples with His ability to calm a storm at sea (Luke 8:24) and even raises a young girl from the dead (Luke 8:54). At this point Jesus' reputation as a healer and teacher was spreading across the country. Rumors were being circulated that he might be Elijah, the prophet from the Old Testament who would return just prior to the coming of the Messiah. Others thought he John the Baptist (who had been killed by Herod, see Matthew 14) risen from the dead. Jesus' followers had seen him teach, debate with the religious authorities, comfort the mourning, and heal the sick. Now Jesus was inviting his followers to be more than spectators of the Kingdom of God and to join in God's mission themselves. He empowers them to cast out demons and to heal the sick. Their main focus is to preach about the coming of God's kingdom. This kingdom is a spiritual movement that is breaking into the everyday reality of the world. Jesus tells his followers not to waste their time trying to convince those who will not listen. He tells them to "shake the dust off of their feet," and head on to the next town. In effect, Jesus is telling the apostles to focus on their job of proclaiming the Gospel message and not to worry about people's responses. That is between them and God. In Israel during this time many people's patience with God was growing thin. For centuries they had been persecuted and held captive by foreign powers. People were eager for the Messiah to come. In today's passage we read about a discussion Jesus had with his disciples concerning his identity.

Pray for the Spirit's Insight

Read the Passage

Understanding the Passage

How does Peter answer Jesus' question?

What does Jesus tell his disciples about his future destiny?

Questions for Further Consideration

Who do you think Jesus is?

Related Bible Passages

Mark 8:27-30

DAY 73

Scripture Reading: Luke 10: 25-37

Creation   Covenant   Christ   Church   Conclusion

Overview: Jesus' ministry followed a cyclical pattern of active work with the crowds, private teaching with his disciples, and personal time for rest and relationship with his Father. It is during one of these private times that Jesus asked his disciples what people were saying about his identity. Throughout his ministry Jesus was always more concerned about a person's personal belief than what they knew about others' beliefs. Jesus asks the disciples very directly, "who do you say that I am? (Luke 9:20)." Peter, who often speaks without thinking in the Gospels, answers quickly, "The Christ of God." This time Peter has answered with a clarity that perhaps even he did not understand. Christ, is not really Jesus' name, but is equivalent to the word Messiah. Peter is stating his belief that Israel's wait is over; the Messiah has arrived. Immediately, in response to Peter's declaration, Jesus tells the disciples to tell no one about his true identity. In telling his disciples to keep his identity a secret, Jesus may have been trying to avoid cutting his ministry short before the time was right. Then Jesus explains to the disciples the divine plan that will eventually lead to the triumph of the Kingdom of God. However, it was not a plan any faithful Jew expected in relationship to their Messiah. The Messiah was supposed to be a figure of power, not one that would be, "rejected by the elders, chief priests, and teachers of the law, and be...killed (Luke 9:22)." While Jesus informs the disciples of this plan several times during the course of his ministry, they never seem to understand it. In today's passage we read about Jesus' encounter with an expert in the Old Testament.

Pray for the Spirit's Insight

Read the Passage

Understanding the Passage

What question does the religious scholar ask Jesus?

What does Jesus think of the scholar's answer to his own question?

Questions for Further Consideration

What is the meaning of the parable of the Good Samaritan?

Related Bible Passages

Mark 12: 28-34

DAY 74

Scripture Reading: Luke 15: 11-31

Creation   Covenant   Christ   Church   Conclusion

Overview: In the previous passage the religious scholar seems genuine when he asks Jesus, "What must I do to inherit eternal life?" In traditional Jewish style Jesus replies to the scholar with another question. The teacher answers with a classic summary of the teaching of the Law, "Love God and love your neighbor." Jesus affirms the scholar's answer and encourages him to live it out. However, just like people of faith today, the scholar wants to know how this teaching is practically lived out. He asks Jesus to define who his neighbor is. Jesus then tells a parable about a man who is assaulted by thieves and left on the side of a country road to die. Interestingly, the first two men who pass by are religious leaders. One is a Temple priest and the other a Levite, an assistant to the priests. Neither of these men help the wounded man. The hero of the story is a Samaritan. Samaritans were considered foreigners and half-breeds by the people of Israel. In some ways they were more despised than even the Romans. By making the Samaritan the person who kept the Law and loved his neighbor, Jesus was once again pointing to God's plan to work His will through all people. In addition, because touching a dead body would result in ceremonial impurity, (Numbers 19:11) the priest and Levite may have refrained from helping because they didn't want to go through the hassle of getting clean again. Here Jesus is pointing out that when religious teaching gets in the way of mercy, something has gone wrong. In today's passage we read another parable taught by Jesus.

Pray for the Spirit's Insight

Read the Passage

Understanding the Passage

Who are the main characters in this parable?

What do you think Jesus is trying to teach through this parable?

Questions for Further Consideration

Is the older brother's attitude about his father's mercy justified?

Which character in the parable can you most relate to?

Related Bible Passages

Matthew 18: 10-14

DAY 75

Scripture Reading: Luke 17: 20-37

Creation   Covenant   Christ   Church   Conclusion

Overview: Biblically speaking, everyone is a sinner (Romans 3:23) but in Jesus' day certain kinds of people were viewed as notorious sinners. Generally, these were men and women on the fringes of society; those engaged in sexual sin and thieves. Religious teachers and people were not supposed to associate with such individuals. One of the major criticisms leveled against Jesus by his opponents was that he associated with sinners, instead of remaining in the company of the righteous (Luke 15:2). In the previous passage Jesus is telling a parable about a lost son to emphasize God's love for all people, especially those who are far from Him. In the story there are three major characters. The first is the father who represents God, the second is the youngest brother who represents a lost sinner, and the third is the older brother who represents Israel or perhaps the Pharisees. The father is generous and extends forgiveness to his lost son. The older brother isn't happy about this and complains that his younger brother is getting a party for being a loser (Luke 15:10). Sometimes, believers lose sight of the fact that the community of faith exists to reach out to the spiritually lost. The church can become an insiders club where we are offended by the idea that someone else, who hasn't been as loyal as we, will be rewarded and embraced by God when he or she finally comes home to faith in Christ. Some Bible teachers have called this the parable of two lost sons because the younger brother was lost outside of the community of faith while the older son was lost within the community of faith. In today's passage we read about Jesus' teaching about the coming of the Kingdom of God.

Pray for the Spirit's Insight

Read the Passage

Understanding the Passage

Will the coming of the kingdom be easily predicted?

In this passage where is the kingdom of God according to Jesus?

Questions for Further Consideration

What two Biblical events does Jesus compare the coming of the kingdom with?

Related Bible Passages

Matthew 24:37-39

DAY 76

Scripture Reading: Luke 19: 28-44

Creation   Covenant   Christ   Church   Conclusion

Overview: Jesus' central teaching during his ministry was on the coming of the Kingdom of God. It was a difficult and elusive teaching for the crowds and even his own disciples to understand. Many faithful Jews believed that the coming Messiah would overthrow the chains of Roman occupation and usher in a golden age of political, economic, and spiritual prosperity for Israel. However, according to Jesus, the Kingdom of God has broken into the world with his birth and ministry. The kingdom was now (Luke 10:11). Every person must make a personal decision to be part of the kingdom or reject it (Luke 10:16). This kingdom is God's remedy for the consequences of the events in the Garden of Eden (Genesis 3). When sin entered the world, after Adam and Eve's disobedience, a worldly, or ungodly, kingdom was allowed to rule in the world. The kingdom of God is the movement that is slowly restoring God's reign over the world. Yet, while the kingdom was present in the Jesus movement it had not yet reached its full realization. This already, not yet, nature of the kingdom is a major theme of the Bible. In the previous passage Jesus is talking about what the Old Testament referred to as the Day of the Lord. On this day the kingdom of God will be fully restored and established. Eventually, this spiritual kingdom will fully break into the physical realm ushering in God's rule over the world. However, until this time, the Kingdom of God begins inside the hearts of individuals as they respond to message of the Gospel in the person of Jesus. In today's passage we read about Jesus' beginning the final part of his earthly ministry.

Pray for the Spirit's Insight

Read the Passage

Understanding the Passage

In this passage does Jesus make a private or public entrance into Jerusalem?

What is the reaction of the Pharisees to this event?

Questions for Further Consideration

As Jesus looked at Jerusalem from the distance he was crying; why?

Related Bible Passages

John 12:12-19

DAY 77

Scripture Reading: Luke 19: 45-48

Creation   Covenant   Christ   Church   Conclusion

Overview: Jesus has spent the majority of his ministry teaching in rural Galilee. His ministry began slowly with the calling of a few disciples, but quickly exploded into a massive movement of the common people. Not everyone followed Jesus through the highs and lows of His ministry, but he had attracted the attention of the religious and secular authorities. The religious leaders in particular were threatened by this traveling teacher who taught ordinary people using stories and metaphors from their daily life. On several occasions Jesus had challenged them and condemned them for what he described as false religiosity (Matthew 23). Jesus had been doing more than teaching the lessons of the Torah. Some of his statements seemed to go against the Law. He broke many of the customs and teachings regarding ceremonial cleanliness and Sabbath keeping. He was also a faith healer and had performed countless miracles throughout his travels. The rumors about this man were in wide circulation claiming that he was a prophet, John the Baptist resurrected, or perhaps even the Messiah himself. When Jesus entered Jerusalem riding on a donkey, the fears of the religious leaders must have been confirmed. Such an entrance, with people waving palms and laying down their cloaks, was the customary welcome for a king (1 Kings 1:33). Jesus was claiming to be the Son of David and claiming his kingship over Israel as he entered the capital city. Some of the Pharisees, who were present for this celebration, asked Jesus to shut down the event but he refused (Luke 19:39-40). Jesus weeps as he looks at Jerusalem, probably contemplating the future that awaits him there. In today's passage we read about Jesus' actions in the Temple.

Pray for the Spirit's Insight

Read the Passage

Understanding the Passage

What does Jesus do when he enters the temple in Jerusalem?

At this point what do some of the religious leaders want to do to Jesus?

Questions for Further Consideration

What does the passage tell you about Jesus' popularity with the people?

Related Bible Passages

Matthew 21: 12-17

DAY 78

Scripture Reading: Luke 22: 39-53

Creation   Covenant   Christ   Church   Conclusion

Overview: Jesus goes to the Temple and clears out the merchants and money changers. Inside the sacred courts of the Temple a marketplace had been established. Here the merchants were selling the animals necessary for the temple sacrifices. Every faithful Jew was commanded by the Law to make these sacrifices. However, according to many writers of the first century the market inside the Temple became corrupt and faithful Jews were being ripped off with overpriced costs for the animals. Jesus may have been angered that the Law, and ultimately God, were being used to take advantage of people. In addition, many believe that through these actions Jesus was foreshadowing the end of the sacrificial system. In the Old Testament God had established the Temple sacrifices as a means for people to get back into relationship with God (see Leviticus). Jesus in a few short days would make the ultimate sacrifice enabling all people to be in relationship with God. The religious leaders knew from history the kind of danger that a charismatic teacher might cause. Jerusalem was filled with religious pilgrims and visitors from all over the world for the celebration of the Passover. Such crowds in the past had been easily incited to violence or rebellion. While the religious leaders, the Pharisees in particular, had no love for Rome they believed that any rebellious actions started by Jesus would only result in greater tragedy for their country. Moreover, Jesus was usurping their religious authority by claiming to be the Messiah. Making their murderous intentions difficult to achieve was the fact Jesus' popularity with the masses continued to be great (Luke 19:48).

Pray for the Spirit's Insight

Read the Passage

Understanding the Passage

What does Jesus ask his disciples to do?

While praying, does Jesus insist that God relieve him of his future task?

Questions for Further Consideration

Who is the person that betrays Jesus and how?

Related Bible Passages

Mark 14:32-51

DAY 79

Scripture Reading: Luke 23: 26-49

Creation   Covenant   Christ   Church   Conclusion

Overview: After the Temple incident Jesus proceeds to teach the crowds in Jerusalem. While teaching, Jesus, has several encounters with the teachers of the religious law. Eventually, Jesus opponents give up arguing with him because of the clarity and wisdom of his answers (Luke 20:39). Jesus teaches at length about the nature of the Kingdom of God and its relationship to the end of the present age (Luke 21). In Jesus, God was doing something new. Instead of finding God unapproachable, people would now be able to connect to God through Jesus. Many people, who were initially hopeful that Jesus was the Messiah, were disappointed with his actions. Jesus was not the kind of Messiah that they expected. Jesus was concerned with the present welfare of his people, but ultimately his message was about a spiritual reality, the kingdom, that changed the way people should live and relate to the world. Perhaps this is why Judas Iscariot, one of the twelve apostles, agreed to betray Jesus to the religious authorities (Luke 22). Perhaps Judas was simply trying to force Jesus to publicly declare his identity. Whatever the human reasons were the Bible also points to the influence of Satan on Judas' decision (Luke 22:3). In the ministry of Jesus the spiritual DNA of the world was being re-fashioned. As Jesus prayed he felt the weight of all the spiritual forces of the world. Yet, he did not demand that God rescue him but set an example for all of us in prayer and life when he said, "Not my will, but yours be done (Luke 22:42)." Jesus willingly goes with the authorities when they arrest him in the middle of the night. In today's passage we read about Jesus fate at the hands of the religious and secular authorities.

Pray for the Spirit's Insight

Read the Passage

Understanding the Passage

How is Jesus killed?

What does Jesus say before breathing his last breath?

Questions for Further Consideration

Is everyone present at this horrific event mocking Jesus?

Related Bible Passages

John 19:17-37

DAY 80

Scripture Reading: Luke 24: 1-12

Creation   Covenant   Christ   Church   Conclusion

Overview: After Jesus is arrested he is brought before the Jewish religious authorities. The High Priest asks Jesus if he is the Son of God, to which Jesus replies, "You are right in saying that I am (Luke 22:70)." Such a response was the ultimate spiritual sin in the eyes of the religious leaders. By declaring himself to be God's son, Jesus was declaring his own divine status. To declare oneself as divine was the worst sort of idolatry possible. This was not acceptable, and in the minds of the religious leadership, impossible. The High Priest and others wanted Jesus killed for his high crime of religious treason. However, under the Roman law they were not allowed to execute anyone. So they took Jesus to Herod (the ruler of Galilee) and eventually to Pontius Pilate, the Roman governor of the entire province of Israel. At first Pilate had little interest in getting involved in a debate of religious ideas. Eventually, he reluctantly agreed to sentence Jesus to death by crucifixion so as to avoid a riot. Many of Jesus disciples had fled or abandoned him at this point. Peter had initially followed Jesus when he was arrested but then denied even knowing him three times (Luke 22:54-62). Some of the disciples, mostly women, were present watching Jesus being crucified. The majority of the crowd, however, mocked Jesus and taunted him with insults. Finally Jesus utters, "Father, into your hands I commit my spirit (Luke 23:46)" and then dies. In that moment the hopes of many were crushed. The spiritual forces of darkness breathed a sigh of relief, for it appeared that the great project of the kingdom of God had collapsed forever. In today's passage we read about certain events that occurred at Jesus' tomb three days after his death.

Pray for the Spirit's Insight

Read the Passage

Understanding the Passage

Who are the first people to discover the empty tomb?

While at the tomb, who do the women meet?

Questions for Further Consideration

Do the male disciples believe the words of the women?

Related Bible Passages

John 20:1-8

DAY 81

Scripture Reading: Acts 1:1-11

Creation   Covenant   Christ   Church   Conclusion

Overview: Jesus' ministry is brought to an end by capital punishment. No doubt many lost their faith in Jesus upon his arrest and subsequent crucifixion. According to the Gospels, several strange events accompanied the death of Jesus, including unusual darkness, an earthquake, and the curtain of the temple being torn in two. Later, Joseph of Arimathea a Pharisee, and member of the Jewish ruling council, obtained the body of Jesus and laid it in his own tomb (Luke 23:52-53). Some of Jesus' female disciples initially came to prepare the body with ointments for burial but had to stop their labors because of the Sabbath. Jesus was dead. However, three days after his death some women returned to the tomb to finish preparing the body. They were shocked to discover that the stone covering the entrance was rolled away and the tomb was empty. They encountered angels who informed them that Jesus was not dead, but alive! (Luke 24:6). The women were astonished and rushed back to the rest of the disciples. Initially, the apostles do not believe the women, but came to believe in the women's words when Jesus' himself appeared to them (Luke 24:36). In Jesus, God re-connected humanity and divinity. The problem of sin, which began in the Garden of Eden (Genesis 3), was now solved. In the past, believers had to make sacrifices to reach out to a holy God who while powerful, seemed distant. In Jesus God became knowable and touchable to all people, Jew and Gentile alike. Death, a consequence of the Fall was now defeated because through Jesus anyone could have everlasting life (John 3:16). In today's passage we read about Jesus' final earthly appearance to the discipleship community.

Pray for the Spirit's Insight

Read the Passage

Understanding the Passage

For how many days did Jesus teach his disciples after the Resurrection?

Who or what does Jesus tell the discipleship community to wait for?

Questions for Further Consideration

What job does Jesus give the disciples to do across the world?

Related Bible Passages

Luke 24:50-53

DAY 82

Scripture Reading: Acts 2:1-13

Creation   Covenant   Christ   Church   Conclusion

Overview: After his resurrection, Jesus taught and instructed the disciples about the Kingdom of God for forty days before returning to God the Father. Not everyone who had followed Jesus before his death continued to follow him after his resurrection. Some believed, some doubted, and some must have stopped believing in Jesus entirely. During these last days of his earthly ministry, Jesus instructed his friends and followers about their job. In the Gospel of Matthew Jesus taught the disciples what is now known as the Great Commission, "All authority in heaven and earth has been given to me. Therefore, go and make disciples of all nations, baptizing them in the Father, and of the Son, and of the Holy Spirit, and teaching them to obey everything I have commanded you. And surely I am with you always to the end of the age (Matthew 28:18-20)." The mission that Jesus gave to the disciples was to be his witnesses all around the world (Acts 1:8). A witness is someone who tells what they have seen and experienced. Jesus asked each of his followers to share their story of faith with others. Remember, the disciples were a small group of people. Most of them weren't very well educated and had spent their whole lives in the rural parts of Israel. Jesus' charge to them must have seemed intimidating or even impossible. Jesus knew that such a mission would be impossible for the disciples by themselves. So Jesus informs them to wait in Jerusalem until God the Father sends the person of the Holy Spirit. The Holy Spirit is the active presence of God who guides believers to do God's will even today. In today's passage we read about the coming of the Holy Spirit at Pentecost.

Pray for the Spirit's Insight

Read the Passage

Understanding the Passage

What appears above the heads of the disciples?

Who can understand what the disciples are saying?

Questions for Further Consideration

What are some of the reactions to the disciples' behavior?

Related Bible Passages

1 Corinthians 14:1-25

DAY 83

Scripture Reading: Acts 2:14-36

Creation   Covenant   Christ   Church   Conclusion

Overview: As promised, the Spirit descends upon the early discipleship community giving them the ability to speak in different languages. The reason so many nationalities were present in Jerusalem was because it was the Jewish celebration of Pentecost (Leviticus 23:15-16). To observe the festival required going to the Temple. When the Spirit descended upon the disciples like tongues of fire, they ran out into the street. It is here the disciples realized that they were being supernaturally gifted to speak in the languages of the world. In this act the discipleship community began to fulfill Jesus' mission of being witnesses to the world (Acts 1:8). The coming of the Spirit showed that God's promise to Abraham to bless all nations was being fulfilled in the new community of Jesus. The reactions of the crowds to this supernatural event were mixed. Some were interested in learning more about the new Jesus movement. Others disregard the disciples as drunkards who babbled incoherently. Historically, some Bible teachers have understood this event as evidence of God's kingdom repairing the damage from the Fall. Back in Genesis God scattered the peoples of the world by confusing their languages at the tower of Babel (Genesis 11). At Pentecost God provided a common language for the whole world to bring them together, the Gospel message of Jesus Christ. Pentecost also affirmed that the discipleship community would not be alone in carrying out the mission of Jesus, the community would be empowered by the Spirit. In today's passage we read about the Apostle Peter, now the leader of the discipleship community, preaching a sermon to the assembled crowd.

Pray for the Spirit's Insight

Read the Passage

Understanding the Passage

What Old Testament prophet does Peter quote in his sermon?

How does Peter connect King David with Jesus?

Questions for Further Consideration

According to Peter, who is Jesus?

Related Bible Passages

Matthew 22:41-45

DAY 84

Scripture Reading: Acts 2:42-47

Creation   Covenant   Christ   Church   Conclusion

Overview: During Jesus' earthly ministry, Peter had been brash and slow to understand the message of his teacher. In the previous passage we see that the events of the resurrection and ascension of Jesus and the descent of the Holy Spirit had changed Peter's life. Inspired by the Spirit, Peter understands the events happening around him as fulfilling the words spoken by the prophet Joel (Joel 2:28-32). In fact, Peter sees the entire Jesus movement as the continuation of God's story from the Old Testament. Jesus is the long awaited descendent of King David that has come to restore Israel. Jesus is the Messiah. In this sermon we see the hallmark of early Christianity, which passionately proclaimed that Jesus was alive (Acts 2:24). The Bible tells us that many people were moved by Peter's sermon. They wanted to respond and Peter challenged them to "repent and be baptized." According to the book of Acts three thousand people became followers of Jesus in response to Peter's message (Acts 2:41). What is amazing about the early church is how quickly it grew. It started as a small group of Jewish men and women who had been Jesus' disciples. Empowered by the Spirit, these men and women began to spread the Gospel message to others who had never known Jesus in the flesh. The early Christian movement was characterized by a strong emphasis on community life and spirituality (1 Corinthians 12:12-30). Individuals had to decide for themselves whether or not to accept Jesus, but once they did, they entered a community of fellow believers. In today's passage we read about the common life of the early church.

Pray for the Spirit's Insight

Read the Passage

Understanding the Passage

What four things did the early Jesus community commit themselves to?

How did the early believers help each other out financially?

Questions for Further Consideration

From the passage can you tell if this way of life was attractive to others?

Related Bible Passages

Ephesians 4:1-16

DAY 85

Scripture Reading: Acts 3:1-10

Creation   Covenant   Christ   Church   Conclusion

Overview: Commitment to Jesus as Lord was synonymous with commitment to the community of disciples in the early church. There was no separating faith in Jesus from participation in Jesus' faith community. Entrance into the community, as well as spiritual growth, required individual effort, but it was all directed toward bringing the people of God together. The book of Acts tell us that the early church was dedicated to four foundational practices. The first was the proclamation and learning of the apostolic teaching. The second was the building of significant relationships with each other. The third was the regular celebration of the Lord's Supper (established by Jesus at the Last Supper, Matthew 26: 17-30). The fourth foundational practice was that of prayer. Christian communities today need to ask themselves if they are building upon these foundational practices in life together. As individuals we need to ask ourselves if we are fully participating in each of these areas. The early Christian community was also marked by a spirit of generosity. We cannot tell specifically from Scripture whether believers gave up personal property entirely or whether they liberally used their personal resources to help each other. While not directly stated in the previous passage, another mark of the early Christian community was joy. The men and women who encountered Jesus through the power of the Holy Spirit were excited about their new way of life. The way of life lived by the early discipleship community must have been compelling because the Bible tells us, "the Lord added to their number daily those who were being saved (Acts 2:47). " In today's passage we read about Peter's encounter with a crippled beggar.

Pray for the Spirit's Insight

Read the Passage

Understanding the Passage

Where were Peter and John going when they encountered the beggar?

Does Peter give the beggar anything?

Questions for Further Consideration

Do you hear any echoes of the Gospels in this passage?

Related Bible Passages

Acts 5:12-16

DAY 86

Scripture Reading: Acts 5:17-32

Creation   Covenant   Christ   Church   Conclusion

Overview: The early disciples of Jesus continued to honor the teachings of the Law and even worship at the Temple. In the previous passage the apostles Peter and John are going to the Temple for a prayer service. Along the way they encounter a crippled beggar who supports himself on the generosity of people going to worship. Peter tells the beggar that he doesn't have any money but that he does possess something else. Peter has faith in Jesus Christ and in his name the apostle heals the beggar. The beggar rejoices along with all of the people present (Acts 3:8-10). This incident echoes dozens of healing encounters that Jesus had with the sick and crippled in the four Gospels. Just as Jesus had empowered the disciples to share in his earthly ministry (Luke 10:1-16), God was equipping the disciples through the Spirit to continue Jesus' ministry after his ascension. Not all of the disciples were given the gift of healing, but all were empowered by the Spirit to carry out Jesus' mission in the world. A goal of the Christian life is Christ-likeness. This likeness is not meant to achieve for us a divine status but to allow God's Spirit to work in our lives, like it did in Jesus, to encourage, bless, and help others. The Jesus movement, led by the preaching and healing apostles, quickly got the attention of the religious authorities. Not everyone was excited about this movement that seemed to be pushing the boundaries of established religion. Many opposed the movement, but the Spirit had come and it wasn't going to be stopped. In today's passage we read about a meeting between the apostles and the chief priests and teachers of the law.

Pray for the Spirit's Insight

Read the Passage

Understanding the Passage

Why do the Sadducees arrest the apostles?

How are the apostles freed from jail?

Questions for Further Consideration

How do the apostles respond to the council's directive not to teach in Jesus' name?

Related Bible Passages

Hebrews 7: 11-28

DAY 87

Scripture Reading: Acts 6: 8-15

Creation   Covenant   Christ   Church   Conclusion

Overview: The Sadducees (who were the temple priests) arrested the apostles out of jealousy and had them thrown into a public jail. The next day they called together the Jewish ruling council, called the Sanhedrin, to discuss the matter of the apostles. Miraculously, an angel of the Lord freed the apostles during the night. Once again the transformative power of the Gospel is evident in the apostles' lives. When Jesus was arrested a few months prior they fled in fear. Now, empowered by the Spirit, they do not go into hiding but return to the temple and continue teaching; a very bold move since the temple was under the jurisdiction of the Sadducees. During the council meeting the elders are informed of the apostles' location. They are then forced inside to appear before the Sanhedrin. On a previous occasion the religious leaders had instructed Peter and John not to teach in Jesus' name (Acts 4:18). Accused of breaking this order, the apostles reply, "We must obey God rather than men!", a response that no doubt infuriated the council. Then loyal to Jesus' command to be witnesses, Peter goes on to explain to the council who Jesus was and that He still lives. The council is unsure of what to do. They dismiss the apostles for a time and discuss the matter privately. Ultimately, they take the advice of a famous Pharisee named Gamaliel. He suggests to the council that they let the apostles go because "if their purpose or activity is of human origin, it will fail. But if it is from God, you will not be able to stop these men; you will only find yourselves fighting against God! (Acts 5:38-39)." In today's passage we read about another disciple of Jesus, named Stephen, and his encounter with the religious authorities.

Pray for the Spirit's Insight

Read the Passage

Understanding the Passage

According to the passage what is God doing through Stephen's life?

What tells you in the passage that Stephen is a gifted preacher and teacher?

Questions for Further Consideration

Are the accusations made against Stephen true?

Related Bible Passages

Matthew 26: 57-68

DAY 88

Scripture Reading: Acts 7: 37-60, 8:1-3

Creation   Covenant   Christ   Church   Conclusion

Overview: Having been let go, the apostles continue their work of witnessing to the resurrection of Jesus. The needs of the Christian community were growing as the number of believers increased. In fact, a sharp disagreement arose regarding the distribution of food to widows. The apostles in their wisdom declared that, "it would not be right for us to neglect the ministry of the word of God in order to serve tables (Acts 6:2)." So what they did was to appoint seven godly men to the important ministry of supporting the widows (Acts 6:3). This was a wise move by the apostles because they recognized that their unique gift was the ability to share the teachings of Jesus. Taking care of the widows of the community was also important, but would not be the best use of their gifts. Stephen was one the original seven men that were set apart for this important ministry of service. Stephen's zeal for God and the supernatural power that accompanied his ministry began to be well known. Many of Stephen's enemies challenged him verbally. However, the Bible says that no one could stand up against Stephen's wisdom because he was being guided by the Spirit (Acts 6:10). This is important detail to note because in the Scriptures and the best of Christian history individual preachers were considered effective not because they were elegant orators but because the Spirit was guiding their ministry. Stephen's enemies then bring him before the religious authorities. They bring false witnesses and make up lies that Stephen is teaching against the Law of Moses and ultimately God himself. In today's passage we read about Stephen's testimony before his accusers and their reaction to his words.

Pray for the Spirit's Insight

Read the Passage

Understanding the Passage

At what point during Stephen's testimony were his listeners offended?

Do you hear any echoes of the Gospels in this passage?

Questions for Further Consideration

What is the name of the young man who began to persecute the church?

Related Bible Passages

Matthew 10:17-20

DAY 89

Scripture Reading: Acts 9: 1-19

Creation   Covenant   Christ   Church   Conclusion

Overview: Stephen gives a long testimony in which he summarizes the entire Old Testament up through the ministry of Jesus (Acts 7:1-53). Everything he was saying was consistent with the teachings of Moses and the understanding of God's story at the time. However, starting at verse 51 Stephen goes after his listeners accusing them of having hard hearts and persecuting the prophets. The religious authorities are livid at Stephen's accusations. Then, apparently in a vision, Stephen sees Jesus in heaven with God the Father. These words ring as the ultimate desecration of God in the ears of the priests and teachers of the law. The penalty in the Law for such blasphemy was stoning. Stephen is then dragged outside of the city where his life is brought to a gruesome end. During Jesus' earthly ministry he often spoke of the persecution and suffering that his followers would have to endure (John 15:18-25). Stephen, in living and dying, was manifesting a Christ-likeness. Stephen's death by stoning echoes Jesus' death on the cross. Jesus prayed for forgiveness for his enemies and, so did Stephen. Jesus, just before dying, offered his life to God; Stephen, just before dying, offered his life to Jesus. Stephen is generally considered to be the first martyr of the Christian faith. A martyr is someone who dies for his or her faith. The previous passage points out that the "witnesses laid their clothes at the feet of a young man named Saul (Acts 7:58)." Saul was a religious leader of the school of the Pharisees. He was in favor of Stephen's death and began to lead a movement of persecution against the church. In today's passage we read about Saul's journey to Damascus.

Pray for the Spirit's Insight

Read the Passage

Understanding the Passage

Why was Saul heading to Damascus?

Who does Saul meet on the road?

Questions for Further Consideration

What is Saul's ultimate response to the events described in this passage?

Related Bible Passages

Acts 22:3-16

DAY 90

Scripture Reading: Acts 10: 1-15, 23-28

Creation   Covenant   Christ   Church   Conclusion

Overview: Initially, the Jesus movement was a small sect within 1st century Judaism. Many Jews were joining this movement whose central message was that the Messiah had come, been killed, and was raised from the dead. Saul, a young and zealous Pharisee, took it upon himself to oppose this threat to the teachings of his fathers. Saul was well regarded by his peers and elders because of his high regard for the Law, his devoted lifestyle and because he had studied under the famous teacher Gamaliel. Saul had been empowered by the religious authorities to hunt down followers of the Way. The Way was one of the first names of the early Christian movement, which echoed Jesus' own words about himself, "I am the way, and the truth and the life (John 14:6)." Saul was on his way to Damascus to find Christians, which he would arrest and have brought to trial. However, along the road Saul is suddenly blinded and has a supernatural encounter with the risen Jesus (Acts 9:5). He remains blind and must be led into the city. There, a disciple of Jesus, named Ananias, restores his sight. Very quickly Saul consents to baptism and commits himself to being a follower of the Way. The life of Saul, who later would be known as Paul the Apostle, is a wonderful example of one of Christianity's central teachings. In the life of Jesus we learn that persecution, betrayal, and even death can be turned around by God to bring new life and resurrection. Saul's life, which was once committed to hatred is transformed by Jesus into a life committed to spreading hope through the Gospel message. In today's passage we read about a vision that the Apostle Peter had regarding who should be a part of the Jesus movement.

Pray for the Spirit's Insight

Read the Passage

Understanding the Passage

How do you know that Cornelius, a non-Jew, is a faithful man?

What does Peter see during his vision?

Questions for Further Consideration

What is the message of Peter's vision?

Related Bible Passages

Acts 11:4-18

DAY 91

Scripture Reading: Acts 13: 1-12

Creation   Covenant   Christ   Church   Conclusion

Overview: The Old Testament Law established several practices which limited the interaction that God's people could have with non-Jews, or Gentiles. By the time of Jesus these initial commandments had been further developed and codified resulting in an almost total separation of Jew and Gentile. Jesus shocked and offended many people by teaching and healing Gentiles. The original plan of the covenant was for Israel to be a priestly nation that would bring God's blessings to all nations (Genesis 12:3). At Pentecost the Spirit opened the door for early Christianity's radical inclusion of people of all races. However, despite the Spirit's leadership at Pentecost, it took the early church a long time to be settled about the issue of including Gentiles. In the previous passage the Apostle Peter experiences a vision of animals which leads him to believe that no one should be called "impure or unclean (Acts 10:28)." The Spirit orchestrates a meeting between a God-fearing Gentile, Cornelius, and the Apostle Peter. Cornelius' faithfulness is obvious because of the supernatural message that the angel brings to him. During the course of Peter's visit Cornelius and his entire household are moved by the Holy Spirit and receive Christian baptism (Acts 10:48). After this event, Peter was criticized by some of the apostolic leadership for breaking the Law by visiting the home of a Gentile. Peter then explains his actions describing the vision he received from Jesus. After this, they rejoiced and agreed with Peter that God was extending the message of repentance and new life even to Gentiles (Acts 11:18). In today's passage we read about the beginning of Saul's ministry as a missionary of the Gospel.

Pray for the Spirit's Insight

Read the Passage

Understanding the Passage

What does the Holy Spirit command regarding Saul and Barnabas?

Do Saul and Barnabas preach only to Jews?

Questions for Further Consideration

What happens to the sorcerer that Paul encounters?

Related Bible Passages

Acts 13:42-49

DAY 92

Scripture Reading: Acts 15: 1-11

Creation   Covenant   Christ   Church   Conclusion

Overview: Following the Spirit's direction, the elders of the church lay hands on Paul and Barnabas empowering them to do the work of preaching the Gospel. The laying on of hands emerged in the New Testament as the sign of the church's affirmation of the Spirit's calling in a person's life. Today, many Christian communities ordain ministers by laying hands on them during a special worship service. It's also important to note that neither Paul nor Barnabas asked to be sent out as missionaries. Their calling came from God and was then confirmed by the church. Barnabas was an important leader in the early church who vouched for the authenticity of Paul's conversion to faith in Jesus (Act 9:26-27). Initially, many people doubted Paul's sincerity because of his history of persecuting the church. Empowered by the Spirit, Paul and Barnabas go preach the Gospel throughout Asia Minor. First the two men go and preach in the Jewish synagogue. This method was one that Paul followed throughout his entire ministry. When arriving in a new town, Paul would first go to the synagogue to preach the message of Jesus. In the previous passage we know that Paul and Barnabas witnessed to Gentiles because the Roman official, Sergius Paulus, comes to faith through their preaching (Acts 13:12). During their visit to Paphos Barnabas and Paul meet a sorcerer named Elymas. Just as in Jesus' ministry, the early Christians encountered supernatural forces that were not of God. Paul, through the power of the Spirit, demonstrates the power of the Gospel over any other supernatural force by causing the sorcerer to become blind. In today's passage we read about an important council meeting of the early church.

Pray for the Spirit's Insight

Read the Passage

Understanding the Passage

What is the disagreement that requires the gathering of a council?

What group of believers are advocating the practice of circumcision?

Questions for Further Consideration

Are disagreements handled in your church like they were in Acts 15?

Related Bible Passages

Ephesians 5: 1-6

DAY 93

Scripture Reading: Acts 15: 12-21

Creation   Covenant   Christ   Church   Conclusion

Overview: The epicenter of the early Jesus' movement was Jerusalem and the region of Israel. However, very quickly, Christian communities began to emerge across the Roman Empire as missionaries like Paul and Barnabas traveled from city to city, bringing with them the message of Jesus. Many Jewish Christians continued to observe the teachings of the Law regarding dietary restrictions and Temple worship. As more non-Jews embraced the message of Jesus the role of the Law in the Christian life became a heated issue. Some believers, who were Pharisees, were teaching that it was necessary to become a Jew before becoming a follower of Jesus (Acts 15:1). Specifically, they were advocating the circumcision of all male converts to Christianity. Circumcision was a primary mark of the covenant that God established with Israel. It began with Abraham (see Gen 17) and continued as one of the essential marks of Judaism through the time of the early church to the present day. Many early church leaders advocated a position that required gentiles to become Jews before accepting Jesus as the Messiah. However, Paul having experienced the Spirit's work in bringing many Gentiles to faith, argued vehemently against this view. Paul would spend a considerable amount of his ministry dealing with issues related to this Jew and Gentile controversy. In almost every one of his letters (often called epistles) you can read a section dealing with this topic. In the previous passage Peter addressed the council advocating a position based on the work of the Holy Spirit rather than the outward observances of the Law. In today's passage we read about the final decision of the council.

Pray for the Spirit's Insight

Read the Passage

Understanding the Passage

James quotes what part of the Bible to support Peter's position?

What does James encourage the council to require of Gentile converts?

Questions for Further Consideration

Do you believe today's church follows the advice of James in verse 19?

Related Bible Passages

Acts 15: 22-35

DAY 94

Scripture Reading: Acts 18: 1-11

Creation   Covenant   Christ   Church   Conclusion

Overview: James, a leader in the Jerusalem church, quotes verses from the prophet Amos to support the position of the Apostle Peter. Across the pages of the Old Testament are various passages that indicate God's concern not only for Israel, but also for the Gentile nations. James is making the claim, like many before him, that the story of Jesus is a continuation of the story of God in the past. Therefore, James' advocates that, "it is my judgment, therefore, that we should not make it difficult for the Gentiles who are turning to God (Acts 15:19)." Instead of requiring non-Jewish believers to observe all of the details of the Law of Moses, he advises that they only be required to not eat food that has been offered to idols, or that is full of blood, as well as to refrain from sexual immortality. These instructions would make racial relationships between different believers easier. For Jewish believers matters of ceremonial purity regarding food were very important. Even though Jesus declared all food as clean (Mark 7:19), some believers still struggled with eating food that had been offered to an idol (Romans 14). If Gentile believers followed these instructions it would be much easier for them to eat with Jewish believers. Today many churches fall into the trap of requiring people to observe certain guidelines or cultural practices before they can become a disciple of Jesus. Many of these practices or cultural attitudes aren't explicitly stated, but are implicitly communicated to new believers. These could range from matters of dress, to receiving a particular level of education, or adopting a particular political position. In today's passage we read about the Apostle Paul's ministry in the Greek city of Corinth.

Pray for the Spirit's Insight

Read the Passage

Understanding the Passage

What was the reaction of the Jewish community to Paul's preaching?

Did any gentiles respond favorably to Paul's ministry in Corinth?

Questions for Further Consideration

What message does Jesus communicate to Paul?

Related Bible Passages

1 Corinthians 1:1-17

DAY 95

Scripture Reading: Acts 28: 17-30

Creation   Covenant   Christ   Church   Conclusion

Overview: Paul's usual strategy of spreading the Gospel was to visit a major city and preach the Gospel. Once some Jews or Gentiles responded and became disciples of Jesus, Paul would instruct them further in the Christian life. Some of these first converts would then become the leaders and teachers of the new discipleship community in that city. Through his many letters Paul continued to encourage and teach these new communities as he continued his journeys. Sometimes Paul would return and visit some of the churches he founded. In the previous passage we read about Paul's ministry in the Greek City of Corinth. As was his custom, he began his work by preaching and teaching in the local synagogue. However, the Scriptures tell us that the Jews in that city were unresponsive and even abusive (Acts 18:6). This hostility motivated Paul to focus his ministry on the gentiles in the city. In the midst of what must have been a difficult situation, Paul receives a message from Jesus. In this vision, or time of prayer, Jesus tells Paul that he will be protected from any harm while in Corinth. Paul's ministry met with success as many gentiles, and some Jews, came to faith in Jesus. Paul stayed in Corinth for over a year to help establish and strengthen the new Corinthian church before continuing his missionary work elsewhere. By establishing communities in major cities, most of which were along major trade routes, Paul was multiplying his efforts in spreading the Gospel. This is because many of the new believers would travel for business and bring the message of the Gospel to other places across the Roman Empire and even into Asia. In today's passage, we read about Paul's ministry in the capital city of Rome.

Pray for the Spirit's Insight

Read the Passage

Understanding the Passage

What was the reaction of the Jewish community to Paul's preaching?

Did any gentiles respond favorably to Paul's ministry in Corinth?

Questions for Further Consideration

What message does Jesus communicate to Paul?

Related Bible Passages

Philippians 1:19-23

DAY 96

Scripture Reading: Revelation 1: 1-8

Creation   Covenant   Christ   Church   Conclusion

Overview: While a pivotal figure in the growth of the early church, Paul was not alone in spreading the Gospel. In fact, he appears to have always worked with teams composed of Jews and Gentiles, as well as men and women. Jesus had commissioned the disciples to spread His teachings around the world (Acts 1:8). A variety of ordinary men and women responded to this extraordinary call with the help of the Holy Spirit. However, conflict among leaders was not unheard of during the early years of the church. Disputes ranged from matters of belief, like in the Council of Jerusalem (Acts 15), to personality conflicts, like that which occurred between Barnabas and Paul (Acts 15:36-41). The marked difference between the efforts of God's people in the past was that, despite human weakness the Kingdom of God continued to spread. Through his life Jesus had made it possible for humans to be agents of God's love despite their personal sin. Paul committed himself to proclaiming this message all over the Roman Empire. His adventures included angry mobs, personal beatings, and being ship wrecked on an island (Acts 27). Repeatedly, Paul got into trouble with religious and secular authorities (Acts 25). By birth Paul was a Roman citizen, a distinct advantage in the Roman world, and a status that he exploited for the benefit of his ministry (Acts 16:37-40). In the previous passage Paul is under house arrest in Rome waiting to appear before the Emperor. What happened to Paul after this event is not entirely clear. Church tradition tells us that Paul, like most of the apostles, was eventually killed for his belief in Jesus. In today's passage we read about another apostle of Jesus who was imprisoned for his faith.

Pray for the Spirit's Insight

Read the Passage

Understanding the Passage

Does the passage give you any hints that it is describing the future?

How does John receive this message?

Questions for Further Consideration

What does Jesus claim about himself in this passage?

Related Bible Passages

Matthew 24:30

DAY 97

Scripture Reading: Revelation 4: 1-11

Creation   Covenant   Christ   Church   Conclusion

Overview: The Roman Empire tended to ignore the religious life of its citizens as long as they paid their taxes and honored Caesar. The Romans considered the emperor to be a divine son of the gods, and a basic expression of civic loyalty was to declare that Caesar was Lord. It was this last matter that the early church refused to participate in. Building upon the Hebrew Bible, the early Christians knew there was only one God and that to worship other gods was idolatry (Deut. 5:7-8). Secondly, a basic profession of faith in the early church was to declare that Jesus was Lord. Over time, the authorities saw this new religious movement as a threat to the stability of the Empire. Many Christians refused to worship Caesar declaring that there was only one Lord, Jesus Christ. The conflict between the kingdom of the existing world order and the emerging reality of the Kingdom of God was a daily struggle for the early church. It was a struggle that involved suffering, persecution, and in many cases death for those who chose to remain faithful to Jesus. The Apostle John, then an elderly man, was imprisoned on the island of Patmos for his faith in Christ (Revelation 1:9). While there he received a vision from Jesus about "what must soon take place." This vision described in symbolic language the end of God's story and provided hope for a church that was being persecuted. Jesus told in the beginning of the vision, "I am the Alpha and the Omega." In other words, despite the present circumstances of life, Jesus will have the final say in this universe. In today's passage we read more about the vision that John experienced.

Pray for the Spirit's Insight

Read the Passage

Understanding the Passage

Who do you believe is the figure sitting on the throne in heaven?

What are the elders and living creatures doing around the throne?

Questions for Further Consideration

How does the worship service of your local church reflect this passage?

Related Bible Passages

Psalm 47:8

DAY 98

Scripture Reading: Revelation 21: 1-14

Creation   Covenant   Christ   Church   Conclusion

Overview: After John's vision, he receives messages for the seven churches in Asia minor that he was overseeing. Each message was tailored to the unique situation of each local church (Revelation 2-3). From their initial writing until the present, Christian communities have found these chapters helpful in understanding their own strengths and weaknesses. After this, John is invited up into the throne room of heaven (Revelation 4:1). Here he observes a majestic scene with a powerful figure on a throne, worshipping elders, and strange creatures with assorted heads and multiple wings. The figure on the throne is described as being radiant with light and the colors of the rainbow. In John's vision this figure represents God Himself. The ultimate reality of God is so beyond the understanding of humanity that even in John's vision God remains a powerful mystery. The elders and living creatures represent the attitude of worship that angelic beings and believers should have toward God. Notice that the elders, wise and powerful as they are, cast their crowns at the feet of God (Revelation 4:10). Revelation is a book that describes the final conflict between good and evil in powerful imagery and world-shaking events. The shorthand word for this kind of literature is called apocalyptic. In addition to being an apocalyptic work, Revelation is also a book describing the nature of authentic worship. Whatever worship style a congregation might worship in, it should be a time for human beings to praise God and cast the crown of their achievements at the Lord's feet. In today's passage we read about the full realization of the Kingdom of God.

Pray for the Spirit's Insight

Read the Passage

Understanding the Passage

Do you hear any echoes of the book of Genesis in this passage?

What happens to those who are not faithful to God?

Questions for Further Consideration

What relational metaphor is used to describe the church?

Related Bible Passages

Matthew 25:31-46

DAY 99

Scripture Reading: Revelation 22: 1-6

Creation   Covenant   Christ   Church   Conclusion

Overview: After the vision of the throne room Revelation describes the last battles between good and evil (Revelation 5-20). The descriptions of plagues, destroying angels, and horsemen are all consistent with the apocalyptic language used by some of the prophets (Ezekiel 6) as well as Jesus himself (Mark 13). Two great themes can be found throughout the Bible that describe the nature of God. One is the theme of God's loving kindness, grace, and forgiveness. The other theme is of God's judgment, discipline, and desire for justice. Each of these themes can be found powerfully in the Old and New Testaments. The tendency for most churches and individuals is to choose one theme over the other as being true. However, the Bible presents both themes as being true of God's story. The tension of living between these two themes is evident in the book of Revelation. Different churches interpret the details of the book of Revelation in radically different ways. The majority acknowledge that its central message is the final triumph of the powers of good over the forces of evil. It points to the final day when Christ will return and usher in the fullness of His kingdom. According to the previous passage, those who refuse to walk in God's ways will not be part of the Kingdom of God (Revelation 21:8). In addition, the last passage echoes the book of Genesis powerfully with its description of humanity and God living together. At the end of God's story the relationship between God and humanity will be fully consummated. The harmony between humanity and divinity will surpass even that enjoyed by Adam and Eve in the Garden of Eden. In today's passage we read more about the details of this coming final reality.

Pray for the Spirit's Insight

Read the Passage

Understanding the Passage

Who is the Lamb described in the passage?

Where else have you read about the tree of life?

Questions for Further Consideration

What curse is this passage referring to?

Related Bible Passages

Isaiah 66:17-25

DAY 100

Scripture Reading: Revelation 22: 7-21

Creation   Covenant   Christ   Church   Conclusion

Overview: The Christian life does not promise prosperity and success while we are living in this fallen world. In fact, it could be argued that a commitment to Jesus Christ as one's Lord and Savior will make life more difficult. This is because a commitment to the Risen Messiah will require choosing Kingdom values over the values of this world. Revelation, while containing descriptions of God's judgment and the fate of those who refuse God's love, should not be viewed principally as a book of doom. Ultimately, the final chapters of God's story will be characterized by the reign of peace and love. The Lamb described in the previous passage is no other than Jesus himself. In the Old Testament a lamb was the principal animal used in the Temple sacrifices. At the Cross Jesus became the sacrificial offering for all of humanity. Jesus' life and death made possible an active relationship between God and humanity. Yet, even after Jesus' resurrection human continued to struggle with sin in a fallen world. In the final reality of the Kingdom the curse that began at the Fall will be broken. Sin will be no more. The tree of life, which was originally in the Garden, will be the center piece of God's dwelling with humanity. Jesus himself declared that no one will know when the final day of the Lord will come. We must strive to be faithful to God's will regardless of when Christ may return. It could be today, next month, or several thousands years from now. The truth is that each of us has but one life to live. We must strive to find out how our personal stories fit into the greater story of God. By doing this we will be confident that our lives have purpose now and in eternity. In today's passage we read the final paragraphs of the Bible.

Pray for the Spirit's Insight

Read the Passage

Understanding the Passage

When do you think Jesus will return?

What echoes of previous Bible passages did you hear in this reading?

Questions for Further Consideration

After reading the story line of the Bible who would you say Jesus is?

Related Bible Passages

Psalm 150

Conclusion

Hopefully, if you're reading this sentence, you have completed all 100 daily readings in the book. You've explored the basic plot line of God's story as recorded in the pages of the Bible from the book of Genesis all the way through the book of Revelation. The goal of this book was to increase your Biblical literacy, and, most importantly, give you a big picture view of what the Bible is about. At this point I imagine you still have many unanswered questions about the Scriptures and about God. This is a good thing. A healthy spiritual life is marked by a lifelong commitment to growing in a personal understanding of the Bible and how it relates to your daily life. You'll find that your grasp of the Bible will grow over time as you expose yourself to it through personal reading, group Bible studies, and preaching.

Right now, you still may be confused as to the relationship between different parts of the Bible. Think about your journey with the Bible like moving to a new area of the country. At first you have no idea how to get anywhere. Then slowly, sometimes painfully, you learn new streets and highways. Over time you slowly start to understand which roads connect to other roads. Sometimes you'll go for months or years then; suddenly you realize a new connection related to the geography of the area. This is what its like with the Bible. You may not understand a particular theme or story right now, but over time the puzzle pieces of Scripture will start to fall in place for you.

The Story of God

Just as a refresher, let's review the basic movements of God's story. In the beginning, God created a wonderful world (Creation). This world was intended to be a place where humanity and divinity lived in perfect relationship. However, human beings chose their own way over God's way which brought sin into the world. Sin is anything that separates us from God, from each other, and ourselves. Then, God made a promise to a man named Abram, who became the patriarch Abraham (Covenant). Through Abraham's descendants God promised to bless all of the nations of the world. After Abraham, came Isaac and Jacob and from this family emerged the people of Israel. God chose this nation to be His people and made a special covenant with them. Through Moses God gave them the Law, which provided instructions and guidelines for living a holy life. The Law was intended to keep human beings and God living in a intimate relationship. However, despite God's faithfulness in the desert and in the Promised Land, the chosen people were not faithful to the covenant. Even the line of kings that God established upon the people's request was mostly unfaithful to the Law. The prophets continually challenged the people to get right with God. For the most part the people did not listen.

Then one day as predicated by the prophets, a descendent of King David came to Israel (Christ). The king was Jesus Christ. He wasn't the kind of Messiah that the people were expecting. He was chiefly concerned with the coming of the Kingdom of God and the implications the Kingdom had for living life. He was not only the Messiah but the Son of God. In Jesus, God restored humanity and divinity into a perfect relationship. In Jesus God gave a free gift to humanity enabling them to stay connected to divinity despite their sin. On the Cross Jesus defeated, and in the Resurrection showed God's desire to transform all death and darkness into something life-giving. The gift of authentic life now and forever is made available to all who accept Jesus as their Lord and Savior.

After Jesus ascended to the Father, the Holy Spirit came upon the early discipleship community (Church). It quickly grew, becoming a movement not only of faithful Jews but of Gentiles as well. Despite persecution and suffering the Church continues to witness to the Gospel of Jesus Christ to this day. According to the Scriptures, someday Jesus will return and usher in the fullness of the Kingdom of God which will include the creation of a new heaven and a new earth (Conclusion).

Next Steps

Depending on your background, you may feel like you've just gotten your feet wet with spiritual things and the Scriptures. To continue to grow spiritually requires a regular diet of Bible reading. I'd suggest, that if you haven't already done so, read through one of the four Gospels (Matthew, Mark, Luke, John), because they will give you a detailed view of Jesus' life and ministry. In addition, the Scriptures were written to, and put together by the power of the Holy Spirit, for a community. They were meant to be understood in a community. If you're not connected to a local church, this would be a good time to go find one. If you are a part of a local church, take advantage of any opportunities for Bible study. Lastly, I want to remind you that God is the master storyteller of the universe. Right now God is weaving billions of smaller stories together, the stories of our lives, into one great story for all time. I challenge you to continue to pray and read Scripture, seeking the ways in which the story of your life fits into the greater story of God.

Printed in the United States
93527LV00006B/47/A